Stops
along the
Journey
of an
Itinerant
Preacher

JOY
IN THE
NIGHT

DON WEST

TEACH Services, Inc.
P U B L I S H I N G
www.TEACHServices.com • (800) 367-1844

Copyright © 2014 Don West
Copyright © 2014 TEACH Services, Inc.
ISBN-13: 978-1-4796-0296-4 (Paperback)
ISBN-13: 978-1-4796-0297-1 (ePub)
ISBN-13: 978-1-4796-0298-8 (Mobi)
Library of Congress Control Number: 2014930957

Published by

TEACH Services, Inc.
P U B L I S H I N G
www.TEACHServices.com • (800) 367-1844

Contents

For my parents, Clement and Darien West, who are gifts from God,
and by whose belief, prayers, and encouragement
I have been kept in the way of the Lord.

Acknowledgments

I have the deepest appreciation for several individuals who selflessly sacrificed their time to read through all or part of this manuscript and offer invaluable feedback. Their suggestions and advice have improved the work in a significant way. These distinguished persons include: Pastor Ryan Simpson, Martin Hanna, Tina Steenmeyer, Pastor Anthony Reid, Balvin Braham, and my good friend and scholar, Adrien Charles-Marcel. Their kind labor is surely noted in heaven's books.

I am also indebted to my mother, whose enthusiasm prompted me to put in an extra few hours of work on this manuscript on several occasions.

I reserve special thanks for my wife, Tracia, who has been a source of constant motivation since the inception of this venture and has meticulously gone through the entire document, line upon line, sharing precious insight and counsel.

Finally, sincere gratitude to my own little flock of prospective preachers: Tajhicia, Trace, Acia Rhodni, and Don Rodney Jr., who, in their unique way, have provided much inspiration for this project.

Foreword

It is a pleasure and privilege for me to recommend that you take time to read this book, *Joy in the Night*, and I will now share four of the reasons why I am happy to write a foreword to the many wonderful words written in this book.

First, Don West became a dear friend of mine while I was a professor of theology at Northern Caribbean University in Mandeville, Jamaica. I remember well our conversations and prayers together. Our talks with each other and with God were especially intense when he was preparing to travel to Mexico to preach in the televised evangelistic series sponsored by the Inter-American Division of the Seventh-day Adventist Church in 2002.

Second, West is specially gifted by God to be a very effective communicator of the gospel of Christ. He preaches fluently in Spanish and English. Also, as you will see, he communicates the gospel in an equally effective way through the printed page. An important part of this efficiency is his sense of humor that incited me to fits of smiles and chuckles at numerous points during my reading of his manuscript. One memorable moment is his narration in sermon five where he details the extent of his cooking skills as a freshman college student. Appropriate alliteration is another attractive aspect of his writing style, such as when he refers to so-called "friends [who] become fiendish and few," "a man in the middle of a muddle," "powerless platitudes," and "the magnificence of the moment."

West points out in sermon four that "we are here to celebrate the wondrous work of a Redeemer and not the winsome words of a preacher." At the same time, I enjoyed the fact that West does use winsome words when he invites those who have "tried and cried" into the exhilarating experience of "anyhow joy." I myself was transported to Palestine and to the time of Christ when I read about the "lonesome, loathsome, leprous, little man [who] heard a word that stirred up hope in his hapless heart. He heard that Jesus was passing by." Reading this book led me to rejoice in the fact that "where men erect a barricading wall, God installs a door of mercy." Like the early disciples, contemporary Christians need "the lubricating oil of the Holy Ghost … to eliminate … friction … among them." In this way we can prepare to participate when Christ returns in the uplifting experience of "Elijah, the great prophet/

preacher, [as he] was about to board his customized, celestial chariot. He was just about ready for his eternal excursion." Yes, reading the winsome words of West has reinvigorated my faith in Christ.

Third, the messages in the various chapters of this book constitute a significant contribution to Christian thought about suffering and joy, weakness and grace, tarrying and going, sin and salvation. The book highlights "the central theme of Jesus Christ—His love without condition, His patience without condemnation, and His justice without compromise." In these words, West lifts up the glory of the sinless and divine Christ, who has united Himself with our fallen, sinful humanity in order to fulfill God's purpose in our creation and our salvation. The complete picture of how God has accomplished this miracle is beyond our comprehension. At the same time, we are to receive by faith what God has revealed for us and for our children. Therefore, West contends with vigor for the faith that is delivered to the saints through God's inspired Word. Christ took our fallen nature, yet He was not fallen. Christ took our sinful nature, but He was not sinful. He became sin for us, yet He knew no sin. Hallelujah!

Fourth, in addition to sharing the messages given to him by God, West has shared himself by telling the story of how and when these messages came to him. As indicated in the subtitle, this book is also about the "stops along the journey of an itinerant preacher." Reading this book has given me a wonderful opportunity of catching up with the experiences of my friend since the time of our face-to-face interactions in Jamaica. Even if you are meeting Don for the first time through the pages of his book, you will find that his testimony of his "tragedies and triumphs" is a powerful witness about partnership with God, and this will hopefully encourage your own Christian journey. I pray that the reading of this book of powerful sermons will impact your life as it has impacted mine. In the words of West, this impact is "an effect that is as lasting as the Creator's own fingerprint on this universe."

Again, I recommend without reservations that you take time for reading and reflecting on the testimonies and sermons presented in this wonderful book.

Martin Hanna, PhD
Director, MA in Religion
Andrews University

Introduction

The original concept of this publication came about as a result of the demand for copies of a series of sermons, many of which were written and delivered during my junior and senior years in the theology undergraduate program at Northern Caribbean University (NCU). These discourses have been a source of immense inspiration and spiritual stimulation for many who have heard them, and the repeated appeal for them to be made available in print is testimony to just how much the power of God was experienced in their proclamation.

These messages and experiences reflect a preaching ministry that has covered ground in Jamaica as well as other parts of the Caribbean, Central and North America, and China. The subjects dealt with are ecclesiastical, doctrinal, as well as inspirational in nature. That which supplies the common denominator, however, is the central theme of Jesus Christ—His love without condition, His patience without condemnation, and His justice without compromise.

It is not the purpose of this project to take on the multiple mysteries that are to be found in the realm of religion or to instigate inconsequential philosophical debates. The focus is rather to provide Christ-centered answers to the perplexing questions of life from the perspective of my own personal tragedies and triumphs. I also hope to aid the reader in attaining and maintaining a state of readiness for the imminent second advent.

A determined effort has been made to preserve most of the sermons in their original format and conversational style of presentation, without doing violence to the principles that pertain to formal writing. One will readily appreciate, however, that the inevitable variations between live preaching and a written discourse can hardly be totally eliminated. The reader may also observe that on a few occasions, recent experiences have been included, as deemed useful, that would not have taken place at the time when the sermon was presented.

The title of this work, *Joy in the Night*, which is based on the opening chapter, has not been selected lightly. It is a living expression of a personal experience of God's redeeming grace and His power to bring life out of death, triumph out of tragedy, and victory out of apparent defeat. It is a testimony to the inestimable mercy of a

God of second chances and a Savior who succors the suffering.

There can be little doubt that the preaching of God's Word, rightly motivated and executed, remains the most potent medium for the demonstration of His power, and the expression of His ultimate will. And that Word, thus spoken into the heart of the intent listener, has an effect that is as lasting as the Creator's own fingerprint on this universe.

The experience of that sublime effect in the lives of those to whom these messages will be new, and the rebirth of that initial passion in the souls of those who have heard them before, is my prayer and desire for all who turn these pages.

Be blessed.

DRW

Spanish Town, Jamaica

"Must weeping endure all night? Should sobs and sighs be my only allies as I wait for the dawning of the morning?"

Prologue

I have decided, in this opening chapter, to invoke an issue that is, by nature, somewhat singular, if not entirely enigmatic. My intention is to address one of those unspoken questions of the afflicted heart. It came to me in a moment of acute anguish as I struggled in the quest for comfort and assurance during the night of a bitter experience. I had turned to the thirtieth Psalm for perhaps the hundredth time because I wanted to read a text with which I was already more than familiar: "Weeping may endure for a night, but joy cometh in the morning."[1]

Strangely, the sight of those well-known words did not produce the expected result. I felt no better after reading them than I did before. The serenity and confidence I experienced on previous occasions when I turned to this text were absent this time around. What happened? Were these words now so familiar that they had lost the power to comfort? Had I read them so many times that my psyche could no longer probe beneath the prose? I struggled to comprehend my own inability to be comforted—to be cured by a remedy that I had personally tested and proven, and the result was a deepening depression unmatched by any previous crucible that I had endured.

As I tried to collect my thoughts and to reason my way toward some kind of mental repose, I came upon the question that caused this cognitive conflict. There was an issue that my "magic text" appeared not to answer, and that was the question of the

---

1   Psalm 30:5b

night. Joy comes in the morning, but what about the night? As I wait for the dawn of the new day, shall I have nothing but tears? Must weeping endure *all* night? Should sobs and sighs be my only allies as I wait for the dawning of the morning?

This, my friends, is that unspoken question of the afflicted heart. It is the question we do not ask aloud for fear of seeming faithless. We are afraid to obtain the "wrong" answer. Hard as it was, I was forced to confront the crisis. At the end of the struggle, the Word proved once again the winner. From the same scriptural source came the promise of joy in the morning and the assurance of *Joy in the Night* while we wait.

At the invitation of Pastor Howard Grant, a friend and former colleague, I had the honor of sharing this message, or at least a version of it, with the Family of God Seventh-day Adventist Church in Spanish Town, Jamaica. May the blessing experienced then be yours now as you ponder anew this biblical jewel from the psalmist David.

The Message: Joy in the Night

"Weeping may endure for a night, but joy cometh in the morning." Psalm 30:5

I would like to begin this sermon with an important and perhaps unsettling warning. This message is, in a certain sense, an exclusive one. I generally prefer that my sermons be of the all-inclusive sort—that there be found in them at least a pertinent line or two for each hearer. But despite my best efforts, I can provide no such guarantee on this occasion. I am obliged to deliver this homily just as it came to me from the Holy Spirit.

There is nothing in this sermon for people who have no problems. If you fall in the category of those who have no issues, no crosses, no perplexities, no crucibles, then I must apologize from the outset and advise you that what I have to say may not be of much significance to you. Believe it or not, this sermon is biased toward the broken, battered, and bruised.

So just in case you have been bearing some burden, just in case you have had some testing times, just in case your night has been longer than you had anticipated and you are standing on the brink of disaster, I would like to announce that you have come to the right place. There is a word of hope for the hopeless and hapless in this message, and I am happy to be the privileged bearer of the good news.

That there are nights in the life of the Christian should be no surprise whatsoever. That there are crucibles we must confront is a fact with which we are all familiar.

To be honest, the absence of some period of difficulty in the journey of one who claims to walk with God is, indeed, a cause for great concern. After all, have we not been well educated by the Scriptures that "all that will live godly in Christ Jesus shall suffer persecution"?[2]

I do not feel that the average believer is significantly staggered by the mere reality of the night phenomenon. The difficulty with which we have to deal is not so much the reality of the night but the nature of the night. I will explain.

In the first place, nights have a way of being dark. The sun rises in the morning over the distant eastern horizon. Steadily, silently, it makes its march across the azure sky, until at eve when it extends its parting gleams over the landscape, and at long last its lingering light is lost.

That there are nights in the life of the Christian should be no surprise whatsoever. That there are crucibles we must confront is a fact with which we are all familiar.

The invention of electricity is one of the admirable achievements of the modern world, and there are lights whose brilliance is remarkable, if not utterly amazing. But no matter how bright the lights get at night, it is an unavoidable fact that when night comes, it gets dark! Lights created by humankind are powerless to prevent the coming of the night, and when we tend to foolishly trust in their potency, the occasional power outage serves as an apt reminder.

There is a deep darkness that surrounds one faced with a night experience in his or her life. When the night comes, it becomes easy to lose one's way because of the limited visibility. We stumble and fall. And then we get up and attempt to start over, only to stumble and fall again. We suffer the bruising and battering that comes with a consistent effort to walk the rugged road in the darkness of night. At times we yield to the temptation to flip the switch of what appears to be a brilliant solution, only to discover that things are not what they seem. The darkness is then compounded by the sorrow of failure and disappointment.

The other thing about nights is that they can sometimes be really cold. I was made to understand what it really means to face cold nights during my time in the state of New Hampshire in the United States, where the temperature can drop to minus twenty degrees Celsius. I need not tell you, having spent the majority of my life in the sunny climate of Jamaica, this is cold weather! One would even think that

---

2   2 Timothy 3:12

in the tropical climate of my homeland there would be no apprehension of such a thing as a cold night. But even on the island of sea and sun, I have had to endure quite a number of chilly nights, especially during the time I lived in the town of Mandeville. Nights can be cold literally, and more so figuratively, when the warm climate of confidence and composure is replaced by the freezing winds of uncertainty and bewilderment.

It is amazing how crippling this coldness can be. It really dawned on me one winter night when my wife went to the kitchen to prepare a light supper. The temperature in Montemorelos, where we live, was about ten degrees Celsius. About twenty minutes afterward, I walked into the kitchen and saw my wife standing in a peculiar half-squat position, with her arms folded and shivering like someone who had just been doused with a bucket of ice-cold water! Of course, when I was done laughing and teasing her about the quaintness of her appearance, she explained to me what the matter was.

"I can't move!" she said. "I hate when it feels like this. All I want to do is get back in bed until it warms up."

That is the chilling reality of the night. It is interesting to see how one usually alive with activity, buzzing with energy and agility can become easily dejected and disabled when the coldness of life's challenges sets in. You feel as though you can go nowhere. You feel you can do nothing but wrap yourself in the insecurity of your own embrace, trying in vain to muster whatever warmth you can in your solitude.

Besides being dark and cold, nights are often quite lonely. I have discovered that the night can become lonely indeed. It gets really lonely when the smiles of cheer disappear and friends become fiendish and few. It gets lonely when the crowd you are used to walking with decides to no longer walk with you. It gets lonely when the one you love ceases to be the one who loves you and the fountain of reciprocated affection somehow ceases to flow. It gets lonely when the pursuit of your prescribed purpose is dismissed as the token of a loss of direction, and the evidence that you do not know what you are about. It gets lonely when the only one who understands you is you, and your own understanding of yourself is minimal.

The night is lonely when prayers are prayed but answers are apparently delayed. The night is lonely when your supplies are done, and your source of replenishment is gone. The night is lonely when you have tried and cried yet failed to fill the empty void you feel inside.

It does not end there. I was given an arresting reminder some time ago of another disquieting characteristic of the night. One morning I was up before dawn making preparation for a short trip to the city of Monterrey. Our son, Trace (four years old at the time), was asleep in our room, or so I thought! I had no idea that he was wide-awake and coherent enough to have a conversation at that hour, until, without warning, he broke the silence.

"Daddy, why is the night so long?"

I answered, "What do you mean, son?"

"I mean that the night is too long, and I want the day to come now."

"Well, why do you want the day to come so quickly?" I asked.

I smiled and nodded as he gave the predictable response.

"It's just that I want to get up so I can go and play with Tajhicia (his sister)."

Nights are dark. Nights can be cold. There are times when the night is unbearably lonely. But perhaps the most distressing feature of a dismal night is the fact that it never seems to pass quickly enough. Nights can often be very long.

I smiled to myself at the thought of the question posed by a boy of merely four years. Why is the night so long? It is a question that reaches to the very core of our being. And what makes the question stand out for me is not just the story I just told you, but the fact that this question is a not a new one. The investigation of the night dilemma is by no means a novel undertaking. In the book of Isaiah we find the same enquiry, "Watchman, what of the night?"[3] David had asked a similar question in the thirteenth Psalm: "How long wilt thou forget me, O Lord? for ever? how long wilt thou hide thy face from me? How long shall I take counsel in my soul, having sorrow in my heart daily? how long shall mine enemy be exalted over me?"[4]

If we read Psalm 30:5 in reverse, focusing on the second clause of our text and then the first, we will see that joy comes in the morning, but weeping may endure for the night. Why is that? It seems to me that our nights appear longer when we think about the morning. Trace had a hard time waiting for the night to pass because he was anticipating the pleasure of playing with his sister in the morning! And this is natural. It is the thought of Heaven that makes the reality of earth so unbearable. It is the hope of success that makes failure so intolerable. We know that better days are coming by and by. We know that this is not how things ought to be. We know that joy comes in the morning, and so it is natural to ask, "Watchman, what of the night?"

Dark nights! Cold nights! Lonely nights! Long nights! Nights of prohibitive poverty. Nights of brotherly betrayal. Nights of inimical indifference. Nights of deepening distress. What of the night?

What shall be the source of my sustenance until the morning comes? Who will be my shoulder to lean on until the morning comes? How do I "keep a cool head" until the morning comes? Where do I get my inspiration until the morning comes?

In other words, is there such a thing as joy in the night? And if joy in the night is

---

3   Isaiah 21:11
4   Psalm 13:1, 2

truly an achievable goal, why does it seem so far beyond my reach?

Well, that could be due to a number of things. It may be that we have misunderstood and misinterpreted David's words: "weeping may endure for a night." If we take a closer look at these words, we will observe that David is talking about a mere possibility and not an absolute certainty. He said, "weeping *may* endure," not "weeping must endure." If I say to you, "I may see you in the morning," I speak of something that might take place depending on certain specified or unspecified conditions. On the other hand, if I say, "I will see you tomorrow," then it is more than a mere probability. I speak with certainty about something that is planned.

If I understand this text correctly, then I am forced to conclude that weeping for the duration of the night is *not* God's plan! It is not God's plan that we should be victims of our circumstances. It is not His plan that all we should have is sorrow until the morning comes. It is not planned that tears and crying, weeping and wailing, sobbing and mourning should be our only lot as we await the dawn of the new day. God says, "For I know the thoughts that I think toward you, saith the LORD, thoughts of peace, and not of evil, to give you an expected end."[5]

> *It is a mistake to attempt to endure the night without invoking the companionship of the Divine.*

Weeping can cease even as the night wears on. We do not have to cry all night. We do not have to mope and grope all night. We do not have to grumble and groan as the hours march slowly by. We can have joy even in the night of our fiercest battles. It all depends on our disposition.

Then again, there is another possibility that could be inhibitive to our nocturnal joy. It may be that we have not given priority to the presence of the Lord as we go through the night predicament. It is a mistake to attempt to endure the night without invoking the companionship of the Divine.

The disciples of Jesus went fishing one night. Jesus was not with them on the trip. In the morning, they brought back a sad report: "Master, we have toiled all the night, and have taken nothing."[6] Not only will your night be long, but you will also have nothing to show for it at the end of the struggle if the Lord is not with you. The morning will come, but it will still be night for you if the Lord is not in the boat. You may work hard; you may exert the maximum of your energy during your night, but your work will be worthless. Your fervency will be futile if He is not with you. If the Lord is not by your side through your personal invitation, then your result will be no

---

5   Jeremiah 29:11
6   Luke 5:5

different than that of the disciples. "I have toiled all night. I have worked all night. I have spent my all trying to make things right all night, and I have achieved nothing."

On the other hand, if the Lord is with you, then your testimony will be quite different. If He is with you, then you will come to know what this preacher classifies as "anyhow joy." "Anyhow joy" is the joy you have that the world thinks you should not have. It is a joy that transcends your circumstances. It is a joy that accompanies you in the valley of the shadow of death when you realize that you are in the valley, but the Shepherd is with you. "Anyhow joy" is your joy in the night—the joy that inspired the apostle Paul to write, "For I am persuaded, that neither death, nor life, nor angels, nor principalities, nor powers, nor things present, nor things to come, nor height, nor depth, nor any other creature, shall be able to separate us from the love of God, which is in Christ Jesus our Lord."[7]

There is yet another reason why joy in the night does not readily come to many of us. It is eloquently expressed by Elihu, a man who witnessed firsthand the intense suffering of his friend, Job. Elihu made a rather striking observation. He said, "By reason of the multitude of oppressions they make the oppressed to cry: they cry out by reason of the arm of the mighty. But none saith, Where is God my maker, who giveth songs in the night?"[8]

This is an accurate appraisal of the human situation. No other diagnosis could be more precise. The problem is two-fold. Firstly, we fail to recognize God's availability: "Where is God my Maker?" Secondly, we fail to recognize His ability: "who gives songs in the night."

Joy comes in the night when we recognize that God is interested in what we are going through, and that He is with us as we go through our crisis moments. We are reminded through the prophet Isaiah, "But now thus saith the LORD that created thee, O Jacob, and he that formed thee, O Israel, Fear not: for I have redeemed thee, I have called thee by thy name; thou art mine. When thou passest through the waters, I will be with thee; and through the rivers, they shall not overflow thee: when thou walkest through the fire, thou shalt not be burned; neither shall the flame kindle upon thee."[9]

As comforting as this may be, I do not wish to dwell further on this point. The point has already been well made in this sermon. What brings me the greatest delight from the text is the second part of Elihu's declaration—God gives songs in the night.

Now I know that there are some somber songs that have been sung at nighttime—songs of sadness, sickness, and sorrow as well as songs of shamefulness and

---

7   Romans 8:38, 39
8   Job 35:9, 10
9   Isaiah 43:1, 2

sin. However, I do not think these are the songs that are being referred to in this blessed text.

When I think of songs in the night, I think of Paul and Silas. These men were missionaries in Philippi. As a reward for the proclamation of the gospel, they were arrested, scourged, and incarcerated. They had enough to complain about. They had sufficient basis for sustained weeping and sorrow. But in the dark midnight hours, there was heard the sound of singing from their cell. These men confronted their night with a medley of praise that arrested the attention of Heaven. The rest of the story you know very well.

When I think of songs in the night, I think of King Jehoshaphat. He was indeed a man in the middle of a muddle. The Moabites and Ammonites had gathered to make war against Israel. But Jehoshaphat did not panic. Instead, he called a meeting. I can hear Jehoshaphat say, "Ladies and gentlemen, we have a bit of a problem. A vast army has come against us, so we need to make some plans. Now, listen to me brothers and sisters, I know we've had some victories before, but we are going to do things a little differently this time. You won't have to sharpen your swords. You won't need to mend your shields. We won't be needing our artillery this time."

"Well, what do you mean King Jehoshaphat? Do you think you have the time to teach us self-defense tactics? Are we going to use martial arts? Have you seen the army we're up against?"

"No, no, my brothers. No martial arts will be needed—just vocal arts! Get the basses together. See if you can find some tenors. I want you to summon all the baritones. We're going to have a little concert."

Well, it seemed a little strange, but they did it anyway. The Bible says, "And when he had consulted with the people, he appointed singers unto the LORD, and that should praise the beauty of holiness, as they went out before the army, and to say, Praise the LORD; for his mercy endureth for ever." And while the choir was busy singing, the Lord was busy fighting. "And when they began to sing and to praise, the LORD set ambushments against the children of Ammon, Moab, and mount Seir, which were come against Judah; and they were smitten." [10]

I tell you, you do not have to fight your battle yourself. You need no sword. You need no shield. You need no arrow. You need no spear. All you need is a hymnal. You will not need more than a song sheet. You do not even need a good voice. All you need is to sing. And while you are busy singing, while you are busy shouting, while you are busy praising, the Lord will be busy fighting!

I do not care what your night is; the Lord has a song for you. In your night of

---

10   2 Chronicles 20:21, 22

loneliness, there is a song—"What a friend we have in Jesus, all our sins and grief to bear." In your night of sickness, there is a song—"The Great Physician now is near, the sympathizing Jesus." In your night of guilt and shame, there is a song—"Would you be free from your burden of sin? There is power in the blood." In your night of hopelessness, there is a song—"The golden morning is fast approaching, Jesus soon will come."

If you want to have joy in your night, listen to David, and listen to him well. He did say joy comes in the morning, but he also shares a personal secret. He says, "My soul waiteth for the Lord more than they that watch for the morning: I say, more than they that watch for the morning."[11]

That is David's secret. Joy comes in the morning. It is OK to hope for the morning, but I am waiting on the Lord for now. If I wait on the Lord, I can have joy right now. If I wait on the Lord, I can have peace right now. If I just wait on the Lord, the morning will come and find me already joyful. It does not mean the night will not be dark. It does not mean it will never get cold. It does not mean it will never get lonely. It does not mean

> *The secret is not how soon the morning comes; it is who is by my side in the night!*

it will not be long. But in spite of all the obstacles, in spite of all the discomforts, I can still be happy. If it gets dark, He will be my light. If it gets cold, I shall be warm in His embrace. If it gets lonely, He will be my companion. If it gets long, He will be my Keeper.

No matter what happens, Jesus' joy is mine. If the sun rises upon the early morning dew, Jesus' joy is mine. If my brow sweats under the sweltering heat of noonday, Jesus' joy is mine. If the cedar tree casts its stately shadows under the beams of the setting sun, Jesus' joy is mine. And if the sun refuses to shine, and the deep darkness of midnight enshrouds my soul, Jesus' joy is still mine because He—the Fountain of my joy—is with me. The secret is not how soon the morning comes; it is who is by my side in the night! Besides, like Elihu said, "God my maker ... giveth songs in the night!"

---

11   Psalm 130:6

Atlanta, Georgia

"God will not build anything that He does not intend to keep."

Prologue

I sat at my desk inside the feared Robinson Hall—feared, of course, only at this time of the year, or should I say, at this time of the semester. I was writing my final exams for the first semester of the year 2002. The course was Evangelism. "Ah, easy," you might be tempted to think. "That's just about preaching and winning souls for the kingdom." Thankfully, I was smart enough not to be thus deluded. From the first day we sat in that class and our professor made his introductory remarks, we knew we were in for a rough ride. This class was going to be no walkover. It would not be just about visiting evangelistic campaigns and taking notes. But even with this timely appraisal, that semester, and that class in particular, was to become the most exasperating challenge that I would have to deal with during my seminary years.

The challenge came about as a result of three main factors. The first was based upon the structure of the course. Unlike most other classes, the final grade was determined by the student's performance on the mid-semester examination and the end-of-semester final exam along with a research paper. Other courses featured multiple tests or sectionals, which clearly favored the student. The second factor was that during that semester, I was selected to participate in an International Youth Evangelistic Campaign in Mexico, which caused me to miss some classes. Strangely enough, my participation in this program did not count toward my Evangelism course, largely due to the third factor—my professor, sadly, was not given to much concession, reasonable compromise, or sympathy. He did not see how the experience I would gain from participation in this evangelistic outreach could be beneficial to the course in question!

So there I was, stranded in the room of the doomed, faced with the possible embarrassment of failing a course about evangelism. (How would I explain this to any conference president?)

I was in need of a miracle. I could still pass the course, but that would require a score of no less than ninety percent in this final exam. By now you must have a fair idea how easy a feat that would be. Another dark night had descended upon me, and joy was nowhere in sight.

I tried to console and control myself as best as I could. Two and a half hours were allotted for the exam. I had reached somewhere around the halfway point when I came upon the question that would turn my greatest challenge as a student into a testimony I would never forget.

I do not recall with precision the wording of the question on the paper. It had to do with what place God ought to take in the affairs of His church and the family. We were asked to provide biblical support for our answers. Psalm 127:1 came readily to mind, and with it came the assurance that I needed for that crisis moment. God chose that unlikely occasion for assuring me that all would be well.

I proceeded to finish the exam one half of an hour before time, and I passed the course with a very respectable grade! And on top of that, it provided the inspiration for the following sermon. God showed up just in time as my builder and keeper!

I had the joy of sharing this sermon on a number of occasions, but the most memorable of which was a divine hour service at the Belvedere Seventh-day Adventist Church in Atlanta, Georgia. This was truly a Spirit-filled affair, and I was honored to have been invited by my former theology professor, Denton Rhone, senior pastor of the Belvedere Church.

The Message: "Except the Lord ..."

"Except the LORD build the house, they labour in vain that build it: except the LORD keep the city, the watchman waketh but in vain." Psalm 127:1

Some time ago a friend of mine invited me to visit the construction site of her new home. She was, of course, filled with excitement and gratitude for what God had allowed her to accomplish. I was happy for her, and when she extended the invitation, I gladly accepted. As we began to tour the premises, I observed that the builders had made significant progress. We took the stairs and went up to the second floor. There, also, the work had reached quite an advanced state. Now I have to confess that I really don't know much about the art of construction. Apart from a boyhood fascination with architecture that led me to take a class on technical drawing in high school, my exposure and interest in that or any related field was, and still is, extremely limited. But as we walked around in that half-finished house, there was something that even my untrained eyes were able to detect. Someone had made a mistake. Some error had been committed. A section of a wall that had been previously built up was now demolished, and the workers were making preparation for repair.

My curiosity got the better of me. I asked my friend, "What happened there?" She explained that the wall had been knocked down because inferior material was used to build it. She discovered the fault on a previous tour of the site and gave instruction for it to be redone. We completed our tour and got ready to take the long trip home. As our car traversed the long and winding road, I smiled upon reflection of the striking spiritual lesson I had come upon that day.

I know very little about construction, but what I do know is this: in the erection of buildings for whatever purpose, there are certain principles and regulations that must be followed. Every discipline has its protocol, and it behooves the practitioners of that discipline to learn and to adhere to the protocol that is pertinent. A contractor follows or ignores the guidelines that govern the building process, which is to the benefit or detriment of the work accomplished.

Let us apply this principle to another realm. In the erection of spiritual buildings, there are also principles and guidelines; there are rules and regulations that must be followed. If our building is to survive the inclement weather that it will inevitably face, it must be built upon a divine foundation, and it must match the Blueprint that the Master Builder has provided. We follow the Creator's building protocol to our own

> *God desires to protect us. He desires to shield us from the futility of this vanity.*

benefit, and you know what I'm going to say next—yes, we ignore it to our own detriment as well.

There is a double reference to vanity in this text. There is the vanity of the builder who builds without committing his building to God, our Builder. And there is the vanity of the watchman who watches without committing his watching to God, our Keeper.

The Bible describes as vanity any human undertaking that does not ascribe to God His rightful place of number one in all our affairs. The Bible describes as vanity a religion that is not founded upon the commandments of God. "In vain they do worship me, teaching for doctrines the commandments of men."[1] The Bible describes as vanity the pursuit of worldly wisdom, fame, and wealth. "Vanity of vanities, saith the

---

1   Matthew 15:9

Preacher ... all is vanity. What profit hath a man of all his labour which he taketh under the sun?"[2] The Bible describes as vanity the long hours we spend working to physically survive, while we forget the Source of our spiritual survival and sustenance. "It is vain for you to rise up early, to sit up late, to eat the bread of sorrows: for so he giveth his beloved sleep."[3]

I am convinced that God desires to protect us. He desires to shield us from the futility of this vanity. And for that reason, the admonition in our text is given. "Except the LORD build the house, they labour in vain that build it; except the LORD keep the city, the watchman waketh but in vain."

There are two verbs mentioned here to which I'd like to invite your attention for scrutiny. The first is "build." The second is "keep." There are also two symbols that are employed by the writer. The first is "house." The second is "city." The house is built, and the city is kept. Both tasks are done in vain if not done by the Lord. These two symbols are of profound interest to me. First of all, if I may ask—what is a house? Someone might say that a house is a place where people live. That is quite an accurate response, but I'd like to suggest a less official and more general definition. A house is a building that has been erected for a particular purpose.

Now I'm not sure whether this was the writer's intention or not, but if we look closely enough, we might just be able to see an interesting connection between the house and the city. If we use the words house and building interchangeably, it would not be hard to see that the house is the basic unit in the city. The city is like an extension, or expansion—something like an immense but unified consortium of houses. A city is what a house becomes after it has been multiplied over and over.

The interesting thing to see is the spiritual application of this house-city connection. You see, the Word of God uses the word "house" to refer to several things. In the book of Matthew, Jesus shares the parable of the man who built his house on the rock and the other who built his house on the sand.[4] In this passage, the house is a symbol of the character of the individual. We are all familiar with Joshua's firm declaration, "As for me and my house, we will serve the LORD."[5] "House," in this case, is a reference to the family. In Mark 11:7, Jesus uses the word "house" to refer to the church, saying that it is a place of prayer for all people.

If the house is the individual character, then the city is the "collective character"—the people of God. If the house is the family, then the city is the worldwide family of God. If the house is the church, then the city is the universal community of

2   Ecclesiastes 1:2, 3
3   Psalm 127:2
4   Matthew 7:24–27
5   Joshua 24:15

faith. However you may choose to look at it, there is that obvious relationship, which makes the psalmist's advice applicable in many situations.

This text of ours declares that God must be the Builder of the house. Obviously, if God is Builder of the house, then He's also Builder of the city. The text says God must be the Keeper of the city. Obviously, if God is Keeper of the city, then He's also Keeper of the house. The obvious conclusion is that, if your house is to be well built, and if your city is to be well kept, then God must be your Builder and your Keeper. I can see why this was an essential concept for the young king Solomon to grasp. Clearly, as one to whom God would entrust the treasures of his wisdom, and as the one honored with the task of constructing the Lord's Temple, Solomon, more than anyone else, needed to know that God is the only one capable of performing that dual responsibility. He needed to understand that God is the only one able to successfully take care of the house and the city at the same time.

You may have a lot of admiration for your leader. He or she may be CEO of your company, president of your conference, or prime minister of your country. He or she may be charismatic, energetic, and diplomatic. But despite the plethora of positive attributes, one person cannot attend effectively to the vast field of responsibility and at the same time attend to the individual interests and inquiries of all his or her subjects. There certainly may be good intentions, but everyone is faulted by the fact that he or she is human, and this humanity locks him or her in a cage of finite confinement. There is no human being who can run the affairs of the house and the city at the same time. Only God can do that! He holds the world in His hands, yet He can still be the friend that clings closer than a brother. He is in charge of the universe, but He's attentive every time I get down on my knees. He supervises all the worlds and their inhabitants, but He finds the time to drop off my meal three times daily, to watch over me both day and night, to stop by my home every morning and evening for devotion, and to build me a custom-made mansion in glory! He builds the house, and He builds the city. He keeps the house, and He keeps the city. It is no wonder that our text says that unless the Lord does it all, all we do is in vain. The question that now faces us is: how well do we follow this admonition?

There are two things with which humankind is predominantly preoccupied; there are two things with which humankind is, by nature, obsessed. There are two things, previously mentioned, that humankind likes to do, which have caused catastrophe, contention, and controversy throughout the history of humanity: we like to *build*, and we like to *keep*!

We like to build. Humanity likes to discover, to create, to establish and bring things into being. And we not only like to build, but we also like to keep. We like to succeed and to continue in our success. We like to create, but we also like to consolidate that which we have created. But the problem with humanity is that we haven't quite gotten things right. Our nature is sinful, our purposes are vain, our motives are selfish, our methods are ineffective, our understanding is clouded, our affections are misplaced, and our self-esteem is often too high. We build, but only so that we can make a name for ourselves. We watch, but only to look out for our own interests. So God says, "Enough is enough. Let Me take over from here. Ascribe to Me the role of Builder and Keeper, and your success is guaranteed."

What then? Is this an excuse for ecclesiastical indolence? Must the church sit back and wait for God to do all the work while we enjoy the Champions' League and the World Cup? Of course not! We are His co-builders. We are His appointed watchmen. And in those capacities we give our service in the building and keeping work of God. We function as the mason, the carpenter, and the electrician. We all work alongside the Chief Designer. We are His watchmen appointed to our specific posts of duty, and our charge is to watch over those entrusted to our care. It is in this manner that the dual responsibility of the child of God is unmistakably defined. God is Builder, but we are His co-builders. God is Keeper, and we are His watchmen.

It would be well if we all took up these privileged positions with equal enthusiasm and zest. Unfortunately, my observations have led to a rather sad conclusion. You see, we get excited about the building part, but we're not too keen on the watching part. Simply put, we like to build, but we don't like to watch. And it's not hard to understand why. With building comes recognition, but with watching comes sacrifice. With building comes praise and admiration, but with watching comes anonymity and solitude. In building, we are on the receiving end, but in watching, we are required to give. Building brings tangible results. With watching, it isn't always so. Watching is demanding. It isn't always comfortable. It cuts into our time. It cuts into our habits, and it often cuts into our budgets. We don't like this watching business too much. It's just so much easier to run a two-week reaping campaign and haul in a few hundred new converts. It's so much easier to write a six-figure check and make a big announcement. Building is easy, and it's rewarding, isn't it? As for watching, well, it doesn't seem to appear on our list of favorite things to do.

But there is a great need that we have in the church today. There is a gaping void that desperately cries out to be filled. It is not a need of builders, but a need of watchmen. Understand me well. I am not talking about those of us who watch because we have eyes. No doubt, at some point in your life you have encountered, as I have, those who continually look away from their own derelict and decrepit edifices to criticize the incomplete construction of another's building. I don't know how they do it, and it leaves me totally flummoxed every time I see it. In themselves they can find no fault whatsoever, but in an instant they can diagnose the sum of someone else's defects. Even Jesus was mystified by this enigmatic phenomenon. "And why beholdest thou the mote that is in thy brother's eye, but considerest not the beam that is in thine own eye?"[6]

I'd like to drop in a word here for anyone who has ever been subjected to unfair criticism or condemnation or prejudice because of the state of your building, or the apparent tardiness of the work. The downward focus of unregenerate onlookers may only enable them to see the broken blocks on the ground, but even those provide evidence that the Builder is at work. It may seem as though not much is happening, but the Builder is surely at work. It takes time to build a house. It takes time to establish a city. If you pause to ponder your position today and make a comparison with your previous predicament, in the depth of your soul you will know that the Builder is at work on the building. He is laying the blocks of character. He's setting the steel of faith. He's mixing the mortar of circumstances. Right now you are merely a work in progress, but soon you will be a finished project—a masterpiece from the hand of your Maker. You are being built in His strength and power. Soon you will be cast in His wisdom, covered with His love, painted in His beauty, and insured by His grace!

> *Right now you are merely a work in progress, but soon you will be a finished project— a masterpiece from the hand of your Maker.*

God is looking for true watchmen—watchmen who do not watch in vain because their confidence is in God, their Keeper. God is searching for watchmen who are not keen to destroy the distraught and to revel in the demise of the fallen. There is an alarming dearth of watchmen who regard their position as a place of humble service, where their primary occupation is to see to the eternal interests of those entrusted to their care. Too many watchmen get carried away by the business of protecting their booths. Too many watchmen are weak and feeble, more willing to be of service to the status quo than to the dictates of the Holy Spirit. Too many watchmen are cold and unfeeling, unapproachable by the young and timid, lacking the simplicity and meekness of the Savior they claim to serve. All this watching amounts to nothing. The booth is occupied, but the citizens are not safe. The cubicle is congested with distracted watchmen while the enemy runs riot within the precincts they ought to protect.

What does God ask of us today? What is the desire that He communicates in these two simple sentences of Psalm 127:1? Though His request is three-fold, it is rather uncomplicated. Firstly, He asks us to work along with Him in the building up

---

6   Matthew 7:3

of His Kingdom. This building work is primarily an evangelistic work, and it is clearly defined in what we have come to know as the Great Commission. "Go ye therefore, and teach all nations...."[7] Secondly, He invites us to be each other's keepers. "Be kindly affectioned one to another with brotherly love; in honour preferring one another."[8] Thirdly, He asks us to invite Him to be our Builder and Keeper.

This, though, is more than an invitation. It is a directive—a directive that must be heeded if success is our desired end. It is a call to total surrender, without which no one can fulfill his assigned purpose in life. This is a divine admonition to dispose of our educated ideas, to dismiss our elevated opinions, and to discard our sophisticated methods. It is a call to give God our all, and to allow Him to be our all in all. To employ the terminology of our text, He must not only be our Builder, and He must not only be our Keeper. But He will be both.

This brings me to my favorite part of this sermon. This brings me to the part of the message that made me almost laugh out loud in that examination room. Two thoughts came to me that day that have never left my mind during the years that have passed since then.

The first is that God will not build anything that He does not intend to keep! As I sat there preoccupied with how my semester would end, the assurance came to me that the same God who was with me at the beginning of the course, the same God who directed in my selection to participate in that campaign, the same God who had issued the call for me to be a communicator of the good news, would help me to finish the race. As Denton Rhone interpreted it, "God honors His commitments." God keeps His promises. He is a God of His Word—a God of integrity. If He doesn't promise it, you can ask for it, but you can't claim it. But if He ever makes a promise, you can count on it. After all, the Word of God does declare, "He which hath begun a good work in you will perform it until the day of Jesus Christ."[9] If you are sure that God was the one who placed you on your present path, you can be sure that He will take you to the desired destination. If you are certain that He was there at the laying of your foundation, you can be certain He will carry the project through to completion. I don't know what the nature of your building is. It may be a relationship or a career. It may be mission project or a business venture. It may be a marriage or the erection of a new church. It may be the literal building of a house of residence. The building doesn't matter. The Builder does. If He started it, He will finish it because God does not build anything that He does not intend to keep.

Secondly, I would have you understand that God will not keep anything that He

---

7   Matthew 28:19, 20
8   Romans 12:10
9   Philippians 1:6

did not build. Of course, you will find this point to be a little less celebratory than the previous. In fact, if you ask me, I think the underlying message is quite sobering and solemn. Have you ever had to ask yourself, "Why is my marriage not working? Why am I not happy with my job? Why does this project seem to be going nowhere? Why do I always feel confused? Why do I fail to succeed even though I pray?" Could it be that you started to pray a little too late? Is there any possibility that you tried to bring God on board after failing to seek His direction at the beginning? Know this—God is our help in time of trouble, but He is certainly no marionette. He will not be an afterthought. If He's going to be with you at all, He will be there from the start. It is said that we plan to fail when we fail to plan, and we can be sure that planning without the Lord is planning to miserably fail. When God is not the one establishing something, we can confidently understand that it is being established by someone else we know very well. If God is to be our Keeper, He must first be our Builder.

I might as well assure you that God is no novice in this building business. He is the ultimate expert in the field of spiritual construction. I should tell you that He not only deals with raising new structures, but He takes care of repairs as well. You may ask how I can be so sure. Well, it's because I am going through a bit of refurbishing myself.

When God says He will be your Builder, He isn't talking about a part-time assignment. If you make Him your Keeper, you can be confident He will be with you for life. He says, "I will never leave you nor forsake you."[10] "Lo, I am with you always, even unto the end of the world."[11]

Make God your Builder, and you will find yourself standing on a sure foundation. With God as your Builder, no inclement weather will be able to destroy your building. The storms of persecution will not be able to blow it down. The earthquakes of rejection will not be able to shake it down. The tornadoes of economic distress will not be able to tear it down. The fires of criticism will not be able to burn it down. If God is your Builder, Jesus will be your foundation, the Holy Ghost will be your Housemate, and the angels will provide security! You're in good company when God is your Builder.

Make God be your Keeper today. With God as your Keeper, you can sing yourself to sleep: "Yea, though I walk through the valley of the shadow of death, I will fear no evil: for thou art with me."[12] "The Lord is my Keeper. The Lord is my shade upon my right hand. The sun shall not smite me by day or the moon by night. The Lord shall preserve me from all evil. He shall preserve my soul. The Lord shall preserve my going out and my coming in from this time forth, and even forevermore."[13]

---

10   Joshua 1:5, NIV
11   Matthew 28:20
12   Psalm 23:4
13   Psalm 121:5–9 (paraphrased).

Malvern, Jamaica

"If the wise virgins sleep, who will warn the foolish?
Who will sound the alarm? Who will keep the lamps burning?"

Prologue

The sermon that follows was first preached at the Malvern Seventh-day Adventist Church in St. Elizabeth, Jamaica. My friend Steve Cornwall had just completed a successful evangelistic campaign, and as part of his aftercare program, he set about inviting a number of student pastors to the church on weekends as a means of encouraging and motivating the new believers.

I remember admiring Steve for taking that extra step that has often been overlooked. He was not just interested in recommending to the church a clear-cut program for follow-up, but he was willing to be a part of its planning and execution. It didn't take long for the results to become apparent. What I found at the Malvern church on that and subsequent visits was an impassioned and vibrant group that was not only excited about what the preacher had to say but also about putting the preacher's preaching into practice.

The sermon, as delivered then, bore an unusual but probing title: "Isn't It Enough That I'm a Virgin?" Over the years, however, it has gone through a bit of homiletic metamorphosis. Yet, the general concept remains unchanged. The same issues are raised.

If there is one thing about which we Seventh-day Adventists have absolutely no doubt, it is the matter of our identity. The word "remnant" is one with which a person becomes familiar almost immediately upon becoming a member, if not before. This, of course, is not at all negative. An understanding of who we are and for what we stand is essential to the efficient execution and completion of our designated mission. There is a certain pride that is productive and provides the unction that is needed to drive us into action. This is useful and necessary, and the lack of it leads to a lassitude, which inhibits true progress and productivity.

The flip side to this pride is arrogance. There is sometimes the proclivity to presume that our identity with the remnant automatically procures for us an invitation to the Bridegroom's wedding celebration. This is, of course, a miserable delusion. It leads to a misunderstanding of our true state and a miscalculation of what it truly takes to be ready for the coming of Christ.

Thus deceived, we eliminate every possibility of experiencing the joy in the night that the wise virgins enjoyed, and all that's left is the inexpressible and irrepressible sorrow that comes with being literally left in the dark.

It should be noted that all ten young women in the parable were, at least in the beginning, friends of the bridegroom. As we can see from the parable, that fell way short of what was required. As I said to Malvern then, I say to you now: it's time to take a serious look at the wisdom of being more than just virgins.

The Message: More Than Just Virgins

"Then shall the kingdom of heaven be likened unto ten virgins,
which took their lamps, and went forth to meet the bridegroom.
And five of them were wise, and five were foolish." Matthew 25:1, 2

They told him to take some more time to think about it. They told him that they thought it was too soon, and that another month or two of waiting would not hurt. They reasoned that he did not know her well enough and reminded him that marriage is a life-long commitment, but their reasoning and pleading fell upon deaf ears. The young man was in love. He was convinced of it. Wedding plans were already finalized, and nothing they could say would change his mind. He went to great lengths to assure them that he'd found the perfect girl. She was born in the church. She was active in youth ministry. She came from a good family and, most importantly for him, she was chaste.

The wedding day came and went. They exchanged vows and rings. They went off for the honeymoon of their dreams. They seemed happy. All appeared to be well.

About six months later the young man ran into a friend at a social gathering. His friend asked, "Man, how are the newlyweds doing? How is your marriage so far?"

The young husband shook his head and looked away as tears filled up his eyes. "To tell the truth, I should have listened to you six months ago. All was well for about a month after the honeymoon. Even then I was sure I had made the right choice. I don't know what has gone wrong, but for the past four months, my wife has turned into a totally different person. She doesn't talk to me with any form of respect. She says she has no interest in having kids. She goes home to her parents every single weekend and has absolutely no clue what it takes to keep a home. I can't believe that someone could change so drastically so soon."

"No sir, no sir," his friend responded. "She hasn't changed. The truth is that you are just getting to know the woman that you chose to marry six months ago."

There is no doubt that the young man in this story was unwise in his selection of a marriage partner. And there is much to be said on the subject of choosing one's spouse well. That, however, is not the subject to which this sermon calls our attention. The focus is on the young woman. To be sure, she had some fine qualities about her, the most outstanding of which was her chastity. This story teaches, however, that as admirable as those characteristics were, as beautiful and untainted as she might have been, there was something essential that was missing.

She was born in the church, but she was not completely converted. She was active in youth ministry, but she was unmoved by her own ministry. She came from a good family, but she didn't learn how to be a good woman. She espoused her sexual integrity, but her heart was far from pure.

The parable under investigation speaks of ten young women. They were no doubt beautiful because they were part of a bridal party. They were no doubt chaste because they were called virgins. These virgins represent those persons in the last days who claim to be anticipating the second advent of Christ, and their purity as virgins depicts their professed faith—a faith that is unique and uncorrupted by error and false traditions.

To the casual onlooker, these ten girls would appear uniform in every respect. They were perhaps similarly dressed. They all appeared to be equipped with the same apparatus. They were all in one place with one purpose—to await the arrival of the bridegroom. They all arose and trimmed their lamps when he came. But among them were some that fell short of something, and although their deficiency was not initially detectable, it would come to light in due time. They were all virgins, but the coming of the bridegroom would reveal that something more was required for admission to the festivities.

I must confess that the reading of this parable has left me in a position of poignant preoccupation for my people and for my church. I must tell you that I am concerned. Not only am I concerned for those around me, but I am also concerned for myself, and the perusal of this passage has led to quite a bit of intense introspection. You see, I have been walking with this band of "spiritual virgins" for quite some time. And it was just recently that I paused to ponder once more my place among this privileged party.

Every now and then one needs to do that. In fact, I'd say a daily review would be wise. It is important to take time to analyze the state of the church and the progress of God's people, but there is also the need for an inward, personal focus from time to time. This message is, primarily, one for the corporate body of Christ, but its powerful appeal has forced me to take the time to look at me, and my conclusion is that there is much preparation and purging yet to be done.

As for the church, the implications are immense and instructive. There are solemn lessons to be learned from this story. Of course, I should make it clear that my intention is not to perform any kind of surgical exegesis on this well-known passage. I simply wish to highlight three points of particular interest.

To begin with, the five foolish virgins traveled with a lamp, but they failed to procure that which was essential to the production of a flame—oil. One can hardly resist the temptation to ask, what were these young women thinking? A ready response comes to mind. Perhaps the issue is that they were not thinking at all! A number of scenarios are possible. It may be that they did not expect a delay, so they assumed that the bridegroom's arrival would precede nightfall, and they would therefore have no need for the use of artificial light. I hardly think, though, that that was the case. Such a theory conflicts with the traditions of a wedding ceremony at the time.

On the other hand, they might have had some oil in the lamps they brought and concluded that what they had would suffice for the night. In this respect they would have underestimated the quantity of oil that was required for the occasion. Another suggested idea is that these virgins were lazy and having failed to make the adequate preparation, received an unpleasant surprise at the time of reckoning.

> *As no lamp can produce light without oil, no one can understand or practice the principles of God's Word without the aid of the Holy Spirit.*

All of this, of course, amounts to mere speculation, but there is no doubt that within the realm of Christianity there can be found individuals, even groups, which fit each of the preceding scenarios. There are those who live their lives based on a certain time when they feel or believe that Christ will return to this earth. There are those who serve God on the basis of "just enough." These make no effort to be totally controlled and filled with the Spirit of God. They merely go through the motions of religion, living on just what they estimate to be necessary to survive from day-to-day. Then there are those who are simply lazy in the spiritual sense. They busy themselves with other pursuits and take no time to invest in the salvation of their souls.

I really do not know what ran through the minds of the five foolish virgins, but what I do know is that a lamp cannot produce light if it has no oil. As one well acquainted with life in the rural setting, I had ample opportunity to learn this bitter lesson while growing up. There were times when a kerosene lamp would run out of oil. There were also times when this happened and we had no money to replenish our supply. On more than one of these unfortunate occasions, I would try valiantly to light the lamp in a desperate bid to dispel the blinding darkness. The wick would burn for a little while and then go out. Then I would turn the handle to expose more of the wick, and light it once more. The same thing happened. The wick burned a while and then the flame died. I should have figured out that in a very short amount of time, we were not only lacking oil but we had also used up the entire wick! Of course, one would readily empathize with my parent's displeasure at such a discovery.

As no lamp can produce light without oil, no one can understand or practice the principles of God's Word without the aid of the Holy Spirit. It was David who helped us to understand what is represented by the lamp. Said he, "Thy word is a lamp unto my feet, and a light unto my path."[1] God, through the movement of the Holy Spirit, inspired the writing of the Bible. As Peter points out, "Holy men of God spake as they were moved by the Holy Spirit."[2] This same Spirit is essential to the interpretation of the Bible. Jesus made that point very clear in the Gospel of John when He said, "When he, the Spirit of truth is come, he will guide you into all truth."[3] Truth may be described simply as what is written in the word of God. As Jesus says, "Thy word is truth."[4]

The results of separating the lamp of God's Word and the oil of the Holy Spirit are clearly demonstrated right before our eyes in the countless confounded factions of the Christian religion, and the pretentious piety of those who are filled with Bible knowledge but devoid of the knowledge of God.

This brings me to what I often refer to as the folly of the wise virgins. We normally confine the folly to the five foolish, who took no oil with them, but I am convinced of my case when I assert that there was a sense in which the wise virgins were foolish in their behavior. The story tells us, "While the bridegroom tarried, they *all* slumbered and slept."[5] We often get so caught up in the wisdom of the wise virgins in being well equipped that we forget to chide them for falling asleep. Was it OK for them to fall

---

1   Psalm 119:105
2   2 Peter 1:21
3   John 16:13
4   John 17:17
5   Matthew 25:5, emphasis added

asleep along with their foolish companions? Do you think they would have gone in with the master had he arrived and found them in that state? I think not. Is it acceptable for the church to lie in slumber while we wait for the coming of the Bridegroom? Is there not work to be done? Are there not foolish virgins naively snoring away in their slumber? Don't we need to warn them? Shouldn't we arise and be alert?

If the wise virgins sleep, who will warn the foolish? If the wise virgins sleep, who will sound the alarm? If the wise virgins sleep, who will keep the lamps burning? Who will shout the last warning to a sleeping world? It is not time to sleep, my friends. Let us wash our eyes with the ice-cold water of vigilance. The enemy stands at the door. The watchman must stand guard. "The night is far spent, the day is at hand: let us therefore cast off the works of darkness, and let us put on the armour of light."[6]

A sleeping church is a church that is excellent at membership expansion but pitiful at membership retention. A sleeping church is one that compromises its standards in order to improve its image. A sleeping church is a church that places more value on its identity than it places on its purpose. A sleeping church is a church that claims Christ's name but lack Christ's compassion.

It is time to arise, not time to sleep. It is time to preach, not time for powerless platitudes. It is time to help, not time to compile impressive reports. It is time to be ready, not time to talk about the wisdom of getting ready. The sleeping of the wise virgins was evidence of their humanity, as many of us will often fail because of our human weakness. But as the bridegroom was merciful to them in the parable, so might Christ favor us if we would now arise from slumber and press on with the work that has been committed to us.

I come now to perhaps the most audacious and foolhardy petition that is recorded in the entire Bible. "The foolish ones said unto the wise, Give us of your oil; for our lamps are gone out."[7] Now, I know not whether to classify this proposal in the category of pure stupidity, blatant effrontery, or woeful ignorance. What I am sure of is that it is certainly one of the most peculiar utterances recorded in the Holy Scriptures! Translated into modern terminology, this is how I think that request would sound: "Brother, give me a portion of the Holy Spirit that you possess because I haven't obtained sufficient for myself." Or perhaps, "Pastor, give me some of the Holy Ghost power that you have because I have run out of my supply." As senseless as it may sound to you, this is, essentially, what the foolish virgins were asking. And the response of the wise was apposite. "Not so; lest there be not enough for us and you: but go ye rather to them that sell, and buy for yourselves."[8]

---

6   Romans 13:12
7   Matthew 25:8
8   Matthew 25:9

Well, as it turned out, the foolish virgins went in search of their own oil. But the Bible tells us that "while they went to buy, the bridegroom came; and they that were ready went in with him to the marriage: and the door was shut."[9]

How unfortunate! They went to do the right thing, but they chose the wrong time. How sad a report this is! And how grave the implication! It is no wonder that the prophet Isaiah issues this solemn warning, "Seek ye the LORD while he may be found, call ye upon him while he is near."[10] The lesson here is that there will come a time when the Lord will not be found by those who seek Him. There will come a time when He

> *Delay is danger, and when the salvation of the soul is at stake, delay can be fatal.*

will not be near. A time had been appointed for the virgins to fill up their receptacles, and a time is appointed to us to obtain the sacred oil of the Holy Spirit. Delay is danger, and when the salvation of the soul is at stake, delay can be fatal.

The Bridegroom will come and find many people running to and fro, trying desperately to prepare at the last minute, but it will be too late. Those who have prepared and patiently waited for Him will be taken to be with Him in paradise, and the door of heaven will be shut. Virgins will be shut out. Many who professed the pure faith will freeze with shock. Many who preached the true gospel will be tortured by their own terror. Jesus painted a very clear picture of the sad scene: "Many will say to me in that day, Lord, Lord, have we not prophesied in thy name? and in thy name have cast out devils? and in thy name done many wonderful works? And then I will profess unto them, I never knew you: depart from me, ye that work iniquity,"[11]

Clearly, being listed among the virgins is not enough. There was no lack of sincerity in the five foolish virgins. There was only a lack of vigilance. There was no lack of good intentions on their part. There was only a lack of good sense. There was certainly no lack of good looks, only a lack of good works. There was no lack of enthusiasm, but there was a lack of empowerment.

If I may, in closing, quote from the inspired pen: "The ten virgins are watching in the evening of this earth's history. All claim to be Christians. All have a call, a name, a lamp, and all profess to be doing God's service. All apparently wait for Christ's appearing. But five are unready. Five will be found surprised, dismayed, outside the banquet hall."[12]

---

9   Matthew 25:10
10   Isaiah 55:6
11   Matthew 7:22, 23
12   Ellen G. White, *Christ's Object Lessons* (Washington, DC: Review and Herald Publishing Association, 1900), 412.

How do we enlist among the right five? We are called to be more than just virgins. We are chosen to be more than just another member of the body of Christ, more than a part of the remnant. We are admonished to be wise—not sleeping, but awake, alert, and tuned in to the signs of the times. Only thus shall we be prepared. Only thus shall we be ready. Only thus shall we avoid the crippling sorrow that will befall those who have no interest in being more than just virgins.

The Virgin Clan

By Don Rodney West

The virgin clan together ran
With fervent strides and lamps in hand
And little thought of looming doom
As on they marched to meet the groom

The sun withdrew its final rays
The bridegroom's coming was delayed
The virgin crew sat down to rest
And by and by they snoozed and slept

Then at midnight the bridegroom came
The foolish trimmed their lamps in vain
"Oh, give us oil!" they begged the wise
"Not so," they said. "It won't suffice."

The foolish five then went to buy
And soon returned with their supply
But oh, too late, the door was shut!
The bridegroom said, "I know you not."

The virgin clan—the remnant band
Must run with oil and lamps in hand
To circumvent the way of doom
As on we march to meet the Groom

Lewis Store, Jamaica

"The will of God is superior to the edicts of mortal men.
Where men erect a barricading wall, God opens a doorway of mercy."

Prologue

If I remember correctly, I had my first appointment at the Lewis Store Seventh-day Adventist Church in St. Mary in early 2002. I found the members there to be a very animated, enthusiastic, and vivacious bunch. If a preacher ever cared about passionate vocal affirmation such as fervent "amens" and "hallelujahs," then this was the place to go. And I will be quick to tell you that this enthusiasm was neither empty nor superficial. This was a group of members who were known for their love of evangelism and their commitment to soul winning, and their efforts were not wasted. This was also the home of a widely respected ministerial colleague and former pastor of my home church in Frankfield, Kevin Danvers, and he was a proven and powerful preacher of the Good News.

I was happy to receive an invitation from the members of the Lewis Store Church to deliver the sermon at one of their baptismal services. When I arrived the Sabbath afternoon for the program, a spirited song service was already underway. A festive and jubilant feeling filled the air. The ambiance was just joyous, and understandably so. In a world darkened by sin and the enemy's deceptions, this small group of candidates had found the Light. A sense of victory pervaded the entire building, and members and visitors alike packed the little church in an effort to share in the proceedings.

I couldn't help it. Before I knew it, I was immersed in the magnificence of the moment. Almost inadvertently I began singing along with the congregation even as I took my place on the platform with the elders. This was certainly not one of those occasions when I had to wait until my turn to speak in order to break the ice and try to arrive at a state of being at ease. No. A few minutes after my arrival I was right at home, with no other consideration on my mind but to be, once again, a mouthpiece for the delivery of the Lord's message.

As I stood up to begin speaking, I quickly scanned the congregation. There were no familiar faces in sight, but there was a familiar Presence. There was no uncertainty in my mind that the Holy Spirit was in attendance, and that His physical presence was the explanation for the spiritually charged atmosphere.

I proceeded to preach a sermon that was conceptualized after a brief study of the intriguing encounter between the Lord and the lonesome leper. The story interested me even more when I read about this particular miracle in Ellen G. White's *The Desire of Ages* and a number of other notable commentaries. It was insightful to see what striking parallels exist between this leper in his infirmity and the state of the human soul.

The twenty minutes permitted only a slight peek into the depth of this story, far less than the spiritual feast that follows; however, it proved sufficient for the moment, if the response during and after the delivery was anything to judge by.

The Message: Lord of the Loathsome Leper

"And it came to pass, when he was in a certain city, behold a man full of leprosy: who seeing Jesus fell on his face, and besought him, saying, Lord, if thou wilt, thou canst make me clean. And he put forth his hand, and touched him, saying, I will: be thou clean. And immediately the leprosy departed from him." Luke 5:12, 13

It is with profound joy that I have accepted yet another opportunity to share a message from God's Word, and it gives me immense pleasure to be able to thus share with this congregation. There are indeed very few settings that bring me as much delight as does a baptismal ceremony. As good as it is to stand in this hallowed place, I cannot afford too much of a preamble, as we are here to celebrate the wondrous work of a Redeemer and not the winsome words of a preacher.

I only have time to tell you a little story. It's a little story of a little man—not that he was necessarily little in stature, but surely he was little in the estimation of his contemporaries. You see, my friends, this little man was a leprous man.

As a consequence of his calamity, he had little accessibility. The towns and villages and society of his loved ones were beyond his reach as a result of his unfortunate expulsion from them. His own home was now, for him, forbidden territory. By the edict of the elders, he had already taken up residence in "Lepersville," the only place where he could pollute no one because everyone there had been already polluted. He had little health, for he was the victim of that which was contagious, contaminating, and contemptible. He had little hope, because he was told that he had what he had because He had angered the Almighty. He was the unfortunate recipient of "the stroke,"[1] and as such, he must live with the repercussions of his putative guilt. This was the tragedy of this lonesome leper.

Then somehow, this lonesome, loathsome, leprous, little man heard a word that stirred up hope in his hapless heart. He heard that Jesus was passing by.

He might have thought, "Who would stop to listen to a repugnant leper? Who would tolerate the stench of my sores? Who would defy the decree of priests and elders? Who would hear the sorry case of one thus banished, destitute, and poor?"

The question may have crossed his mind, but it surely didn't block his path. I'm not sure whether he knew the chorus: "Reach out and touch the Lord as He passes by." I don't know. The record doesn't say. Nevertheless, he embarked upon a journey of faith that would lead him to a moment of miracles.

Let us take note of the manner in which this poor man was described. His diagnosis was not merely that he was a leper, but as the doctor Luke put it in lucid language, he was "full of leprosy." Now, if I may be allowed a humble confession, I do not possess enough faith in my own ability to bring you to a full understanding of what it is that we are dealing with here. Let me therefore defer to the more skillful narrator John Gill, who advances the following description:

The patient's voice is hoarse, and comes rather through the nose than the mouth … The face resembles a coal half extinct, unctuous, shining, and bloated, with frequent hard knobs, green at bottom, and white at top. The hair is short, stiff, and brinded; and not to be torn off, without bringing away, some of the rotten flesh, to which it adheres; if it grows again, either on the head or chin, it is always white: athwart the forehead, run large wrinkles or furrows, from one temple to the other; the eyes red and inflamed, and shine like those of a cat; the ears swollen and red, eaten with ulcers towards the bottom, and encompassed with little glands; the nose sunk, because of the rotting of the cartilage; the tongue dry and black, swollen, ulcerated, divided with furrows, and spotted with grains of white; the skin covered with ulcers, that die and revive on each other, or with white spots, or scales like a fish; it is rough and insensible, and when cut, instead of blood, yields a sanious liquor: it arrives in time to such a degree of insensibility, that the wrist, feet, or even the large tendon, may be pierced with a needle, without the

---

1   Ellen G. White, *The Desire of Ages* (Mountain View, CA: Pacific Press, 1898), 262.

patient's feeling any pain; at last the nose, fingers, toes, and even privy members, fall off entire; and by a death peculiar to each of them, anticipate that of the patient: it is added, that the body is so hot, that a fresh apple held in the hand an hour, will be dried and wrinkled, as if exposed to the sun for a week.[2]

> *If there is one lesson worth learning from the approach of the leper, it is the following: in your quest to find the Healer of your soul, no one can stop you but you.*

Ponder then, dear friends, what a miserable, detestable object this man was. It was said he was full of leprosy, and now you will sympathize, if only momentarily, with the abject terror of the multitude at his approach. There were no doubt some who felt obliged to deter him, but he was resolute and would not listen until he came face to face with Christ.

If there is one lesson worth learning from the approach of the leper, it is the following: in your quest to find the Healer of your soul, no one can stop you but *you*. The resistance of the multitude is not a decent enough deterrent. The brawny, barrier-building disciples are not an acceptable alibi. If you don't make it down to the valley of healing, it's not the pastor's fault. Don't blame the sister or brother, even though you might have suffered many trials by reason of their tyranny. Not that I set out to cause an offense to anyone, but I'm obliged to say that if you somehow don't get to the miracle spot, it's perhaps because you didn't try hard enough.

If I may now make a sobering application from this story, I'd like to point out that there is a very great likeness between this infirmity called leprosy and sin. Isaiah the prophet understood this similitude to the extent that, as he pondered the plight of the Hebrew nation, he could only produce the following report: "Ah sinful nation, a people laden with iniquity ... the whole head is sick, and the whole heart faint. From the sole of the foot even unto the head there is no soundness in it; but wounds, and bruises, and putrifying sores."[3] David, too, lamented his own impurity in similar terminology: "There is no soundness in my flesh because of thine anger; neither is there any rest in my bones because of my sin ... My wounds stink and are corrupt because of my foolishness ... for my loins are filled with a loathsome disease."[4]

As the leprosy defiles and ultimately destroys the body that bears it, so does sin defile the soul and heaves it toward damnation. As the leprosy robs its subject of the

---

2   John Gill, "Luke 5:12," Salem Web Network, http://bit.ly/1dofiG2 (accessed November 14, 2013).
3   Isaiah 1:4–6
4   Psalm 38:3, 5, 7

society of friends and family, so does sin sever the connection between a person and God. And as the leper is hopeless and cannot avoid the approaching demise except by means of a miracle, such is the lot of the sinner, unless the Healer of souls intervenes.

There *was* an intervention in this man's case on that unforgettable day. It was not just for the leper's benefit that Jesus attended to him, but for ours, as this encounter bears with it several lessons for our present edification.

After he had forced open for himself a path to the Healer through the teeming throng, the leper then sought to address the Savior, and did so in this manner: "Lord, if thou wilt, thou canst make me clean."[5] He spoke nine ordinary, uncomplicated words, which communicated at once not only his desire to be healed but also his attitude toward his condition, his aspiration, and his Lord.

His petition was that he be made clean. This means that he understood and had come to terms with his condition. "Make me clean" is another way of saying, "I acknowledge my uncleanliness, and my impotence to rectify it." This is the first step on the path to reconciliation with God. We must be able to say, "I acknowledge my transgressions: and my sin is ever before me."[6]

The Lord does not view with pleasure our efforts to excuse sin and to call it by any name other than what it is. If the patient never considers himself to be sick, then the doctor has no basis upon which to offer healing. The fact is that leprosy is rampant, and we have all been infected. The prince has no fewer sores than the pauper, notwithstanding his reluctance to admit it. A leper is a leper regardless of how he presents himself. Though he may associate himself with spiritual men, as did Gehazi, he yet remains a leper. Though she may thrill the saints with melodious music, as did Miriam, she still remains a leper. Though he may adorn himself in kingly attire and be the proud holder of a high office, as was Naaman, he remains a leper, and he shall be thereby condemned, until he recognizes his sorry status in the presence of a holy God. There is no hope for those who hide their sins, but if we confess them, God "is faithful and just to forgive us our sins, and to cleanse us from all unrighteousness."[7]

Presently, I would invite your attention to a most remarkable observation. It amazes me to note that no matter how intense the leper's suffering was, or how earnest was his petition, he knew that his request must first be vetted by the divine will. Hence the words "if thou wilt." He was submissive to what Christ would do, even if that meant that he continued in his suffering. What childlike submission! What exemplary humility!

Yet I would go even further to suggest a secondary implication of these words.

---

5   Luke 5:12
6   Psalm 51:3
7   1 John 1:9

Lepers were caused to exist under a yoke of imposed guilt. Their spiritual leaders brainwashed them to the extent that they felt hopeless in the sight of God. They were told that the disease on their skin was the result of some hideous sin they had committed, for which there could be no restitution. But when this man said to Jesus, "If thou wilt, thou canst make me clean," it was a testimony to his belief that he was standing in the presence of One who had infinite power. It was as though he said, "I have been condemned by men, but you can remove that condemnation. I have been cursed by my brethren, but if you desire, you can reverse the curse, and instead bestow upon me an infinite blessing. I have been denounced as unclean and discarded to be thus regarded forever, but if it pleases you, you can put to naught the words of pompous men. You can bring forth a clean thing from out of an unclean. You are Jesus the Christ. You have come forth from Nazareth, and if you want to, you can rescind the prognosis of death and speak life into my being once again."

I have seen people written off by other people myriad times; they were denounced as too vile, discarded as corrupt and unredeemable. I have seen souls strive time and again to attain to a place of peace with their God, only to be adjudged pretenders, hypocrites, and imposters by those who often overestimate their own good standing with God. But the will of God is superior to the edicts of sinful beings here on earth. Where humanity erects a barricading wall, God installs a door of mercy. I have seen the devil proven a liar and have often times witnessed the miracle of transformation wrought upon many thought to be without hope. Nothing is impossible with God.

Our infant daughter fell ill one day and was in need of medical attention. We took her to the nearest hospital and asked a nurse as to which doctor it would be best to speak to. We were given the names of about three doctors who were on duty at the time. We chose the one with whom we felt most comfortable, and in good time, the situation was rectified. The truth is that any one of those doctors could have seen Acia, and the result would likely have been just as positive. But when this leper said "Thou canst make me clean," this principle of corporate capacity did not apply. He did not mean to say, "Thou art one of those who can make me clean," but rather, "Thou *alone* canst make me clean." The words that acknowledged Jesus' power also announced humankind's lack of such power. The priests could not but "thou canst." The doctors could not but "thou canst." The magicians could not, and cannot and will not ever be able to cleanse me, but "thou canst make me clean." If we could inject these words into our praying vocabulary, with the same faith and conviction as this leper displayed, we might come to our own moment of miracles and have a life-changing encounter with our Lord. *He can* cleanse the leper. *He can* forgive the sinner. *He can* restore the offender and redeem the backslider to His fold.

At the leper's request, the eyes of all those present must have turned in Jesus' direction. A thousand thoughts could have crossed their minds. Still struggling to overcome the shock that Jesus would even permit a leper to come into His presence, they now watched with bated breath to see the next stage of this peculiar encounter. They knew the rules. They were acquainted with the consequences that were sure to follow for anyone who dared to have physical contact with the victim of this contagious malady. Jesus had the power to heal by speech. I am sure the majority expected Him to use this method. He was the Son of God indeed, but He was God's Son *in human flesh*. Would He risk His own contamination by touching the leper? They did not have to wait long to see. Luke reports, "And he put forth his hand, and touched him, saying, I will: be thou clean. And immediately the leprosy departed from him."[8]

The leprosy would have immediately fastened itself upon any other human being, but it could exert no such power over the Divine Healer. He could not be contaminated by leprosy, but He could end its fiendish reign over its miserable subject. He cannot be contaminated by sin, but He can easily deliver the sinner from its deadly grasp. It was a significant touch, just as the Great Physician has touched sinful humanity. He would not heal us from a distance. The Redeemer has not assumed an aloof stance. But He has indeed touched us by becoming one of us. Not that there weren't other methods at His disposal, but He would have it no other way. Paul could not have stated it more eloquently when he said God "made Him to be sin for us, who knew no sin; that we might be made the righteousness of God in Him."[9]

I don't know if you've noticed, but there was urgency about His response. His reaction to the petition was immediate, and the effect of His touch was instant. You know, you may ask God for some temporal blessing, and the answer might be "No." You may pray about some cherished desire, and He may tell you to wait. But if you come to Him pressed down by some issue of the soul, if you approach His throne with the request that you be freed from sin, and if your petition is "Create in me a clean heart ... and renew a right spirit within me,"[10] I guarantee you this day that there will be no delay. Don't even be shocked if it happens before you can form a prayer on your lips because He did promise through His prophet that "before they call, I will answer; and while they are yet speaking, I will hear."[11] It is not that He cares less about our temporal needs, but there is no need that is greater than our need for salvation, and therefore none that requires greater urgency.

Well then, as we approach the finish line, let me highlight one final detail that is overlooked by a surprising number of commentators. An encounter has occurred

---

8   Luke 5:13
9   2 Corinthians 5:21
10   Psalm 51:10
11   Isaiah 65:24

between the Lord and the leper that has resulted in a separation between the leper and his leprosy. Let us be careful not to miss the manner in which this separation took place. We are told that "the leprosy departed from him." He did not depart from the leprosy, but the leprosy departed from him. He did not depart from it because he could not, even if he wanted to. He was a leper, and the malady clung to him. Everywhere he went there went the leprosy with him; his constant, contemptible, corrupting companion. He had no power of himself to part with it, no matter how much he tried to. In order to be separated from his sickness, it had to be taken from him, a transaction that could only be wrought by miraculous means. Now is it not the same way with the leprosy of sin?

> *As the leper could not leave his leprosy behind on his own, neither can we forsake sin except with God's intervention.*

As I was visiting homes in a community in St. Mary where I was conducting evangelistic meetings, I met a man who spoke of his desire to change his life and to join the church, but who said that he could not at the present time do so because he had a number of habits he desired to break before coming to Christ. I tried my best to explain to him that he would not be able to achieve this despite his best efforts, but he insisted on defending his position.

As the leper could not leave his leprosy behind on his own, neither can we forsake sin except with God's intervention. "Can the Ethiopian change his skin, or the leopard his spots? then may ye also do good, that are accustomed to do evil."[12]

I have never heard that one possessed by a demon got up and walked away from the demon at will. The devil will not so easily let go of his prey. He will not amicably agree to mutual terms of separation. He must be cast out, forcibly, and by none other than the conquering Christ.

Our most zealous efforts to purify ourselves will utterly fail. We cannot save ourselves—not by keeping the law, benevolent acts, dedicated service, or selfless sacrifice. Christ alone can expel the spirit of evil, Christ alone can command the leprosy to depart, and Christ alone can separate sin from the sinner. If we would reach out to Jesus Christ as He passes by, if we would confess our guilt instead if concealing it, and if we would humbly ask Him to purify us as only He can, then He would reach out His hand of mercy to us. He would impart His healing touch, and the leprosy of sin would at once depart. The Lord of the loathsome leper is the Lord of the penitent sinner.

He is more than willing to make us clean.

---

12   Jeremiah 13:23

St. Augustine, Trinidad

"There can be nothing accomplished in which God will delight, that excludes the direction and the benediction of the Holy Ghost."

Prologue

In February 2002, I went to Nuevo León, Mexico, to attend a special training seminar that was hosted by the Inter-American Division Youth Ministries Department. During the one-week seminar that was held on the campus of the University of Montemorelos, I met Kevin Pierre, a Trinidad and Tobago native who was representing the Caribbean Union Conference. We happened to share the same room during our stay in Mexico, and our interaction during those few days became the initiation of a close friendship.

Our conversations often switched into a good-natured wrangle over certain minor cultural peculiarities, but these were readily laid aside in the interest of a greater cause. Indeed, our presence at this special training seminar was indicative of our mutual passion—the proclamation of the everlasting gospel. And though I did not hear him preach during that week, I saw enough to be convinced that he had committed his life to evangelism not merely because of his natural endowment with the gift, but because of his conviction that this was his God-issued mandate.

Prior to meeting Kevin, it had never entered my mind to travel to Trinidad and Tobago, but as is often the case, a substantial interaction with someone from a foreign territory somehow leads to a deeper interest in that place. And thus it was with me. As the week wore on, I questioned my friend about innumerable things pertaining to his homeland. What is the culture like? How are the people? Are there many Jamaicans living there? What is the church like? Are there many young people?

Being a creative preacher not lacking in linguistic luster, Mr. Pierre painted a most inviting picture. At the end of it, not just I, but a number of similarly enthralled listeners vowed to plan trips to the Eastern Caribbean.

I do not know how many of those vows were actually fulfilled, but two years later, during the year-end holiday season, my chance came, and I took it *con mucho gusto* (with pleasure). I was not disappointed, and I found that there was very little exaggeration, if any at all, in Kevin's colorful promotion of his homeland.

Eager to ensure that I made the most of my three weeks, Kevin drafted quite a packed agenda. Apart from day trips to key spots on the island and an invitation to see a traditional wedding, my weekends were to be spent fulfilling preaching appointments in several of the local churches. Though I went to Trinidad primarily as a tourist, it was in the latter that I took greatest delight. My visit to the La Horquetta Seventh-day Adventist Church was indeed memorable, as was my trip to Stanmore Avenue, which was where I delivered the sermon for the new year.

One day, as I strolled through a commercial center in Port of Spain, I had a chance meeting with Pastor Robert Liverpool, a gentleman I had met earlier that year when he visited one of the churches I was serving in Clarendon at the time. He was the executive secretary of the South Caribbean Conference in St. Augustine, Trinidad, and it was at his cordial invitation that I presented the following message during a conference committee meeting. I felt it was a setting suited for a word highlighting the joy of unity in labor with the Holy Spirit.

The Message: An Invitation to Tarry

"Go ye therefore, and teach all nations, baptizing them in the name of the Father, and of the Son, and of the Holy Ghost." Matthew 28:19

"And, behold, I send the promise of my Father upon you: but tarry ye in the city of Jerusalem, until ye be endued with power from on high." Luke 24:49

There are times when I pause to ponder my personal and professional progress and to make a comparison with the priorities that I've prescribed. These periods of reflection have also been useful in helping me to identify some accomplishments that I have *not* made. And if I may be honest with you today, there is one confession that I would like to make.

One of the things that I did not do during my growing up years was to establish myself as a man of the kitchen, or as someone who could be depended upon to perform any remarkable feat in the area of food preparation. I mean, if I were the only partaker, then I could pretty much please myself, but as long as other empty stomachs and salivating mouths were part of the equation, then it was not expected that any major part of the catering would be entrusted to me.

In recent times, though, this has somewhat changed due to a number of factors, the most obvious of which is the economic burden of eating the easy way. This reality forced itself upon me very violently during my time as a university student. It was during my freshman year that the experience I am about to share took place.

I was living in the community of May Day, just below the university, and I was late for work in the Campus Safety Department, where I served part-time. I looked quickly in the refrigerator and grabbed the last egg from the tray. I had just enough time to make a sandwich. I lit the stove, put the frying pan on, poured in the oil, and waited for it to heat. Then I broke the egg and emptied it into the hot oil, just like I had done countless times before. But this time I didn't hear anything, so I thought the oil was perhaps not hot enough. Maybe the stove had gone out. But when I checked, the flame was right there: big, bright, and blue.

"Well," I thought, "that's a little strange. Eggs usually protest a little bit when being fried. Hmm. This is interesting."

At this time, I began to notice a very disturbing aroma coming from the stove.

"Don't tell me this is happening!" I sighed in frustration. "Why must the last egg be a bad one?"

Then, as if guided by some unseen power, my eyes turned to focus on the bottle from which I poured the "oil." I immediately doubled up in uncontrollable laughter. I was trying to fry my egg with *liquid soap*!

Of course, I share that experience today with far less bashfulness than when it had just occurred. That is partly due to the fact that with the passing of time, I have become far less reserved about acknowledging my own gaffes.

> *Our mission will only be accomplished in the way He intends, in the time He ordains, and by the means He provides.*

The more significant reason, though, is that my egg sandwich mishap has provided me with a rather potent spiritual analogy.

As I reflected recently upon this unforgettable occurrence, it struck me that so many of us, as servants of Christ, have been making a valiant effort to prepare a savory cuisine of service for our Lord. And though we may be very skilled and our intentions may be honorable, very often we come up with a flawed list of ingredients. No matter how hard I tried, I could not prepare a palatable sandwich with the ingredients I had.

In the same way, there is no way we can please God by using our own systems, methods, and ideas, whether we attempt to do so consciously or out of ignorance. We cannot fulfill the Great Commission equipped with the tools of our choosing. Our mission will only be accomplished in the way He intends, in the time He ordains, and by the means He provides. Anything short of this will be an effort in futility.

We have been entrusted with a mission, and we have been informed of the means by which it must be accomplished. We are familiar with the mandate, given by Jesus during His final interaction with His disciples: "Go ye therefore, and teach all nations, baptizing them in the name of the Father, and of the Son, and of the Holy Ghost." This divine fiat is for all who would be called Christians. All who enlist among His disciples are enjoined to "go." We must go. We must all go quickly, earnestly, and unreservedly. But before we go, there is something else we must do. Before we go, we must tarry!

Now, before you dismiss this as some preposterous contradiction, I'd like to bring to your attention again these words from Christ: "And, behold, I send the promise of my Father upon you: but tarry ye in the city of Jerusalem, until ye be endued with power from on high." Jesus was very clear in issuing to His disciples their mission, but He was equally clear in advising them that they were not to embark upon it without the outpouring of the Holy Ghost. The success of their mission was dependent, not only upon their response to the commission but also their compliance with this secondary command.

To us modern-day disciples, the same principle applies. I know that the concept of waiting and seeking for the anointing of the Holy Ghost has been twisted and misconstrued by many, but this does not mean that it is no longer relevant to our work or no longer required for our success. The directive to go might have been given before the directive to tarry, but the disciples understood quite clearly that they were not to set one foot outside Jerusalem until they were imbued with power from on high.

The day of Pentecost is often remembered for its numerical significance—3,000 members joined the church. It's hardly remembered, especially in some circles, as the day when the Holy Spirit fell upon the disciples in dramatic fashion. This was the reason for the evangelistic success. Peter did preach a mighty sermon. There was indeed a massive public effort in the city of Jerusalem. But the miracle of Pentecost happened because those disciples had camped out for days inside the upper room, emptying their souls before God, and waiting for the coming of the Comforter.

`Why do I believe that this message is relevant? It's because of an observation that I have made: we are a "going" people but not a "tarrying" people; we are an enthusiastic people but not an empowered people; we are a preaching people but not a praying people; we are a spirited people but not a Spirit-filled people.

Nevertheless, we are instructed that "if divine power does not combine with human effort, I would not give a straw for all that the greatest man could do. The Holy Spirit is wanting in our work."[1]

It is astounding to watch how hard the Holy Ghost must fight these days to obtain admission to the boardrooms of Christ's church. Professionalism and efficiency appear to be preferred these days above spirituality. In fact, it is not advised to present oneself as being "too spiritual," lest he or she become a distraction and turn away the intellectual elite. It is not trendy to speak much of the Holy Ghost, as this will impede the effort to reach the upper class. We cannot afford to alienate the finer minds, it is said. It is considered contrary to good strategy to dwell upon themes such as Pentecost and miracles, healings and tongues, so as not to be confused with the "wrong" movement.

But notwithstanding the new, fashionable way of thinking, I cannot but preach what is in the Word of God. I cannot but declare with passion the things that are written, with the prayer that I be kept from "cunningly devised fables."[2] And if I must be preserved from erring, it is by this same Spirit that I will be, for "when he, the Spirit of truth, is come, he will guide [me] into all truth."[3] Through that guidance I will be able to bring others to the light. Therefore, I have no option but to preach of Him, and by Him, and through Him, and with Him.

There can be nothing accomplished in which God will delight that excludes the direction and the benediction of the Holy Ghost. From the beginning He has worked in tandem with the Father, and He will not desist from so doing through the ages that are to come.

It was by the Spirit that God moved upon the waters at the inception of this world's history. Through the Spirit He communicated His will to the patriarchs and prophets. It was the Holy Ghost's withdrawal that heralded the doom of the antediluvians and condemned Sodom and Gomorrah to their unfortunate fiery fate. It was the Spirit that was represented by the anointing oil by which kings and rulers were separated for sacred service. This same Spirit moved upon Mary, and she brought forth the Messiah. And when Jesus was to enter into His earthly labor, the Spirit descended upon Him like a dove. The Spirit then led him into the wilderness thereafter, and He was sustained for forty days as the Tempter tested Him. And at the end of His ministry, as He was to pass on the mantle, He desired that His emissaries should have access to the same arsenal as did He. So He told them, "Go ye therefore; but before you go, be sure to tarry ... until you are imbued with the Holy Ghost power."

---

1   Ellen G. White, "How to Meet a Controverted Point of Doctrine," *Review and Herald,* February 18, 1890.
2   2 Peter 1:16
3   John 16:13

In other words, Jesus told them, "Don't cook with the wrong oil. Don't set aside divine inspiration for human imagination. Don't replace intercession with informed intuition. Don't confuse professionalism with piety and purity. Make sure you get your ingredients right."

The commission in Matthew is already a well-studied subject. The injunction in Luke is where I want to drop my anchor for now. Why was Jesus so adamant about it? He had not too long before given them the assurance that all power in heaven and earth was His. Couldn't they go forth in that power, even as they had before, and enter at once upon their assigned mission? No; not until they received the divine token indicating that that authority was officially passed to Him, having accomplished His mission during His sojourn among humanity. Consider this: "It is expedient for you that I go away," Christ had said to His disciples, "for if I go not away, the Comforter will not come unto you; but if I depart, I will send Him unto you."[4]

"Christ's ascension to heaven was the signal that His followers were to receive the promised blessing. For this they were to wait before they entered upon their work. When Christ passed within the heavenly gates, He was enthroned amidst the adoration of the angels. As soon as this ceremony was completed, the Holy Spirit descended upon the disciples in rich currents, and Christ was indeed glorified ... The Pentecostal outpouring was Heaven's communication that the Redeemer's inauguration was accomplished. According to His promise He had sent the Holy Spirit from heaven to His followers as a token that He had, as priest and king, received all authority in heaven and on earth, and was the Anointed One over His people."[5]

They needed to tarry for other reasons in addition to the preceding. If you read from John 15:18 through 16:6, you will observe that Jesus had made some rather frightening revelations to His disciples. The cruelty and wickedness that was meted out to Him was to extend to them also as they went about their work.

This news was not a source of joy for them. They had not yet learned how to rejoice at the prospect of persecution. As Jesus observed them, He saw that sorrow had filled their hearts.[6] It was at this point that Jesus gave them the assurance that He would send them Someone to aide them through their journey. The Holy Spirit would supply the comfort that was crucial for the coming crisis.

We need that Comforter today. The work before us is fraught with mountainous challenges. The hazards that we must handle are so menacing that even the bravest among us is sure to fail without His assuring presence. One does not have to look too far to see the challenges the church faces, not only from outside influences but also

---

4   John 16:7
5   Ellen G. White, *The Acts of the Apostles* (Mountain View, CA: Pacific Press, 1911), 38.
6   John 16:6

from within its own ranks. By way of an example, I was appalled only this week by what I heard coming from the lips of two self-styled ministers of the gospel, who were guests on a popular reality TV show. These so-called men of God, speaking to a television audience of millions, had the effrontery to assert that homosexuality is a gift from God. Isn't this taking iniquity to another level?

There are moral and social challenges as well as personal and ethical challenges and even organizational and spiritual challenges. The Comforter is needed to motivate us and illuminate us.

We are members of a movement—not a popular one, but one that is marginalized because of its message, vilified because of its values, persecuted

> *It is true that unity is not always necessary for people to achieve great things on their own merit. But it is equally true that unity is indispensable for us to excel in Christ.*

for its preaching, and slighted because of its standards. It is for this reason that we need all the more to tarry. It is for this cause that we cannot cease to pray, and to pray in earnest, that by the Spirit's power our fears may be conquered and the cause of Christ advanced.

They needed to tarry before they went out, so that the lubricating oil of the Holy Ghost could be poured upon them to eliminate whatever friction remained among them. They could not be used as God's instruments if there was an absence of true peace in the camp.

It is true that unity is not always necessary for people to achieve great things on their own merit. But it is equally true that unity is indispensable for us to excel in Christ. Differences must be dispensed with and all disparity discharged. All competitiveness and striving for supremacy had to be aborted and absolutely abandoned.

We are divided into fields and districts, conferences and unions, not that we might out-perform and out-score each other, but that we might more easily reach every borough and every village, every town and every city, every slum and every suburb, every high hill and every low valley. The record reveals that on the day of Pentecost, "they were all with one accord in one place."[7] That place was the place of prayer and the pursuit of peace and Holy Ghost power, and we are enjoined to go there, and tarry there, until one band of love binds each element together and the glory of God is revealed.

There is yet another reason that they needed to wait upon the Holy Spirit. Through them, God intended to do a reproving work among the people. Jesus told

---

7   Acts 2:1

them, "And when he is come, he will reprove the world of sin, and of righteousness, and of judgment."[8] They dared not attempt to do this without the authority of the Spirit of God, though some today have had the temerity to try. The sinner cannot reprove sin. The unrighteous cannot convict the unrighteous. The condemned cannot preach of judgment to come. The disciples were unqualified for this sacred purpose until the Spirit came, and His presence was the only way to validate their ministry.

It is for these reasons that I extend to all this invitation to tarry. It is an injunction that Christ has already issued. But we have forgotten, and hence, my invitation to consider, once again, the former things. It behooves us to revisit the old ways—the old ways of praying and waiting for answers, then going forth with assurance and power. We need to relive the old ways when the upper room was a place for meeting with God and not for scheming with others, and the old ways when a prayer meeting could be called on any day, and everyone would come—when they would come because there was going to be a communal communication with Christ and not just because there was going to be a speaker of interest.

We are wandering in a woeful spiritual wilderness, and this is not because the Spirit has become less available, but because of a shortage of worthy vessels into which He may be poured. God will not waste His sacred oil, and as long as we continue using the artificial oil of our own wisdom, our own knowledge, our own motives to do God's work, the worthless wheel of failure will roll on and on.

The reality is that we cannot afford to fail. There is too much to do, and the time is too short. There are too many to be reached, and the stakes are too high. We have no choice but to pursue the outpouring of the latter rain.

Let us learn the lesson of Elisha. Elijah, the great prophet and preacher, was about to board his customized celestial chariot. He was just about ready for his eternal excursion, but there was a major matter that moved upon his mind. He was preoccupied about the young prophet from whom he was parting. Having served as God's mouthpiece to Israel, he understood the magnitude of the mission that awaited his intern. But he would not tell him what he needed. He wanted to see if Elisha knew, and if he cared to have it. He said to him, "Ask what I shall do for thee, before I be taken away from thee."[9] Elisha already knew what he needed. It was neither money nor power. It wasn't wisdom or prestige. What he needed was the Spirit of the living God. So he said, "I pray thee, let a double portion of thy spirit be upon me."

How about that! He didn't ask merely for the Spirit, but a double portion of the Spirit. He understood that if he was granted that Gift, then with the Spirit would come a full supply of all his other necessities.

---

8   John 16:8
9   2 Kings 2:9

Let us learn the lesson of Zerubbabel, who, when given the mammoth task of rebuilding the Temple in Jerusalem, was issued this reminder through the prophet Zechariah, "Not by might, nor by power, but by my spirit, saith the LORD of hosts."[10] The temple was surely built by might. Its walls were planted with great power, but not of the human kind. It was the power of the Spirit of God. And this great statesman, as an example to us, enjoyed the success of uniting his effort with that of the Holy Ghost.

We need His help today. We are nothing without Him. We can do nothing without Him. But if we are in Him and He is in us, if we work for Him and He works through us, if we live by Him and He lives in us, if we learn from Him and He inspires us, if we listen to Him as He speaks to us, if we invite Him and let Him fill us, if we look to Him and let Him lead us, and if we will trust Him and let Him use us, then the heavens

> *Tarry we must, and not in wasteful indolence, but in fervid pursuit of His promised presence.*

will open, the latter rain will be poured out, miracles will be wrought, lives will be transformed, sins will be forgiven, joy will come in the night, and Pentecost will be brought forward, from past history to present reality.

Tarry we must, and not in wasteful indolence, but in fervid pursuit of His promised presence. And when He comes, of this we can be sure: He will anoint us and appoint us, baptize us and bless us, convict us and comfort us, dedicate and designate us. He'll empower and energize us, fashion and fortify us, graft us and grow us, humble us and heal us. He will inspire and ignite us, join us and jolt us, kindle us and keep us, lift us and lead us. And if we don't get weary of Him, then He will melt us and mold us, nestle us and nurture us, order and ordain us, purify and prepare us, quicken and qualify us, restore and revive us, saturate and sustain us, transform and transport us. And if we yet permit Him, and give Him full sway, then will He unbind and unbridle us, vindicate and validate us, wake us and warm us; and if we allow Him, He will woo us to work for Christ with a yearning and youthful zest.

There shall be no mountain that before us will not crumble, no demon that before us will not tremble, no sickness that before us will not surrender, and no storm that before us will not subside. Thus may we be in the hands of the Almighty. Thus must we be. The only issue that remains is—are we willing to tarry?

---

10 Zechariah 4:6

Northern Caribbean University, Jamaica

"He's a great psychologist, and a wily strategist,
but it is obvious to me that Satan is a poor biologist!"

Prologue

It goes without saying that one of the most important classes that a theology student must take is homiletics. For this critical aspect of my ministerial development, I was privileged to have the inspiring Denton Rhone as my teacher. I was very pleased when it came my turn to take this class, as prior to it I had very little reason to be confident in any ability that I had as a preacher. I did make a courageous attempt at a one-week revival series some time earlier, but my performance did little to encourage me, much less those who made the daily effort to come out and listen to my sermons. By *those* I mean the members of the Truro Seventh-day Adventist Church in Frome, Westmoreland, who very graciously and patiently bore with me that week, and many of whom remain loyal friends.

During that semester, I also had another source of inspiration. Dr. R. Clifford Jones, who was visiting from Andrews University, conducted our Week of Prayer. His messages were so compelling, so unique, and so awfully moving that I felt obliged to approach my own preaching with an intensified sobriety. It was during that week that I first began to understand just what a sermon is and what it can do under the influence of the Holy Spirit. This was the perfect point of departure that was warranted now that I was about to learn the methodology of rightly dividing the Word.

Needless to say, the course was very effective. Rhone not only excelled in imparting the principles of excellent preaching, but he himself excelled in the pulpit, which made his task that much easier. He believed strongly in a practical approach and was not afraid to put the more promising of his pupils on the stage that they may prove themselves and hone their homiletic skills.

On one occasion during that semester there was an appointment in Kingston that he was unable to meet, and he intended to send me in his place.

I asked, "Did they give you a theme for the program?"

His response: "Don, I want you to pick your best sermon, go to Meadowvale, and preach it with all your heart."

It was not to be, however, as the local pastor recklessly and arrogantly assessed the occasion as being too grand for a "mere student"—an unfortunate instance of the crass and rash treatment meted out by some to younger ministers from time to time.[1]

However, Dr. Rhone, who was also serving as pastor of the university church, had no such reservation when he decided to embark upon an unprecedented preaching project involving three of his students. A divine worship service was planned in which the sermon was to be delivered by a trio of pastors-in-training.

The other speakers were Ryan Simpson, a senior, and Steve Cornwall, a classmate of mine. We were given the theme "Revisiting the Cross of Calvary," and we were instructed to divide the sermon into three sub-themes as follows: Ryan was asked to open by looking at the cross from the perspective of the patriarchs and prophets. Steve was to follow with a recap of Jesus' actual suffering and agony, and my task was to conclude with what it all means for us today.

At the end of the service, our professor and pastor did not hide his pleasure at the success of yet another creative and uplifting divine hour. But his response was only one of many that I quietly observed—some of them marked by tears and others by vigorous handshakes that required no accompanying words. We felt like people were satisfied that they were ministered to, and for me, that is the memory that I've cherished the most.

As it appears here, the sermon reflects only what I was able to dig up from my mental vault, having not exercised as much care as I should have with my only copy. It also carries a new title—"The Little Red Spot," and the motive for this change will become evident upon reading the very first paragraph.

The Message: The Little Red Spot

---

1   The present author rejects the unChristian and erroneous philosophy held by some individuals that a form of "religious ragging" and ministerial marginalization is a necessary part of the development of a youthful minister. It is his conviction that the spiritual connection between Paul and Timothy and the paternal love expressed by the more experienced apostle is a far more acceptable model than the callous methods often employed by a certain misguided class.

"But he was wounded for our transgressions, he was bruised for our iniquities: the chastisement of our peace was upon him; and with his stripes we are healed." Isaiah 53:5

It is said of the French general Napoleon that after the devastating defeat at the Battle of Waterloo, he sat down to meet with a number of his strategists. As they reviewed the colored map before them, Napoleon pointed to a red spot that represented England and said, "Except for that red spot I would be master of the world."[2]

It would not be difficult to imagine Satan in a similar scenario. The only difference would be that he would point to a blood-stained spot called Calvary. I can hear him saying, "Were it not for that little red spot, *I* would be champion of the world today."

Well, friends, the devil did *not* win that battle, and that is only thanks to what transpired at that little red spot on the periphery of the Judean capital. It is to this place that we desire to call your attention today. We invite you to come with us, not because you have not gone there before, but because the more often we visit the place of His passion, the deeper will be our appreciation of Him and what He has done there for us.

The cross of Calvary is the symbol of our eternal redemption. Ever since the moment of its erection upon the ghastly hill of Golgotha, it has remained the ever-present emblem of God's inexplicable love for a rebellious, reprobate, and reckless race. It stands as the token of the amazing grace that has become our story and our song.

This grace is God's selfless gift to humanity. It was not just for those who were witnesses to Christ's earthly deeds. It is not just for those of us who by faith have accepted the testimony of the Gospels, but for those who preceded the fulfillment of the promise—those who lived expectantly for centuries before the birth of the Babe in Bethlehem. Indeed "the grace of God that bringeth salvation has appeared to all men."[3]

It appeared to the first parents, Adam and Eve, who, even before they were issued the verdict for their rebellion, were given the assurance of a plan for redemptive action. They were there to witness what God declared to Satan: "I will put enmity between thee and the woman, and between thy seed and her seed; it shall bruise thy head, and thou shalt bruise his heel."[4] The woman was to bring forth a *Seed*. (Don't forget this!) The serpent was to succeed in bruising Him, but in the process, his temporary dominion over humankind would be terminated, and he himself dealt the blow of death.

---

2   Joe Crews, "The High Cost of the Cross," Bibleuniverse.com, http://bit.ly/L8pLvc [accessed December 6, 2013].
3   Titus 2:11
4   Genesis 3:15

From Adam and Eve to their sons and daughters, and from them right down the ancestral line, the promise was passed with prophetic precision, and the hope for a Deliverer was kept alive.

It was through the family of Abraham that God intended to bring His plan to pass. To the patriarch He said, "In thee shall all families of the earth be blessed."[5] From him, God raised up a nation that was to proclaim to the wider world the designs God had for humankind.

"There shall come a Star out of Jacob, and a Sceptre shall rise out of Israel."[6] These were the words unwittingly uttered by the prophet Balaam, reflecting the expectancy of those who had put their faith in the promised Messiah. And lest they should forget, God, through Moses, implemented the system of the earthly sanctuary. With each lamb that was slain on the sacrificial altar came a sure reminder that there was coming a Lamb of God, whose mission was to take away the sins of the world.

His faithful messengers received the prophecies concerning Jesus with joy, and with the same enthusiasm, they testified of them and waited for their fulfillment.

David was waiting when he declared, "He shall be as the light of the morning, when the sun riseth, even a morning without clouds."[7] Hosea was waiting when he proclaimed, "His going forth is prepared as the morning, and he shall come unto us as the rain."[8] The prophet Malachi was waiting when he asserted, "Unto you that fear my name shall the Sun of righteousness arise with healing in his wings."[9]

But perhaps the most pointed prophecies that pertained to the Messiah and His mission were reserved for the prophet Isaiah. The pen of this gifted poet documented these memorable words: "For unto us a child is born, unto us a son is given: and the government shall be upon his shoulder: and his name shall be called Wonderful, Counsellor, The mighty God, The everlasting Father, The Prince of Peace. Of the increase of his government and peace there shall be no end, upon the throne of David, and upon his kingdom, to order it, and to establish it with judgment and with justice from henceforth even for ever. The zeal of the LORD of hosts will perform this."[10]

The glory of the coming Deliverer would exceed all who preceded Him and all who came after Him. But there was a less rapturous side that this prophet revealed. In his writings are also painted in bold relief the most vivid pictures of the Savior's suffering and sacrifice. Here is outlined in lucid language both the matter

---

5   Genesis 12:3
6   Numbers 24:17
7   2 Samuel 23:4
8   Hosea 6:3
9   Malachi 4:2
10   Isaiah 9:6, 7

and the manner of His messianic ministry. So shocking was that which he had to reveal, and so contrary to the popular hopes and expectations, that he was obliged to commence this part of his narrative with the probing question, "Who hath believed our report?"[11]

It was no ordinary report that he carried. For sure it was the good news, but for those whose spiritual vision was impaired, they were unable to discern the goodness of the news. The testimony of the prophets had largely been rejected by those who heard them—a situation that would not change even when the Son of God walked among men. But whether or not people would believe, the testimony would still be given.

"For he shall grow up before him as a tender plant, and as a root out of a dry ground: he hath no form nor comeliness; and when we shall see him, there is no beauty that we should desire him."[12]

There was to be no grand entry for the coming Prince. The Son of God was to have no regal welcome from His countrymen. He would meekly spring from obscurity like a plant in its infancy, susceptible to the abuse of humanity and nature, with minimal expectation that it would come to prosper or grow to anything of considerable standing. He was not born in a palace, but in a measly stable with the dumb beasts numbered among His welcoming delegation. He was not born to affluent parents, but to a poor carpenter and a simple damsel, hence His lack of form, comeliness, and His comparison to a root out of dry ground. Not that He wasn't majestic and princely in His physical appearance, for He was without spot and blemish as we have come to know. He was indeed the Lily of the Valley, but His circumstances were unflattering, and nothing to attract the attention, like a vulnerable plantlet, or insignificant shrub.

It is no wonder that this testimony was not accepted. It is easy to see why they did not believe. This is not the Deliverer that had been envisioned, which is why the preacher continued to lament, "He is despised and rejected of men; a man of sorrows, and acquainted with grief: and we hid as it were our faces from him; he was despised, and we esteemed him not."[13]

A more fitting term could not be found to describe our Savior—a Man of sorrows. From His lowly birth to His forced flight into Egypt, He was a man of sorrows. From his crude life as a carpenter's Son in Nazareth to His wilderness interrogation with the devil, He was a man of sorrows. From His frequent fights with the Pharisees to His personal preoccupation with His own disciples, He was a Man of sorrows.

---

11   Isaiah 53:1–12
12   Isaiah 53:2
13   Isaiah 53:3

Yet the time would come when His burden of sorrows would grow heavier. The moment would arrive when He would be forced to carry not just His sorrows, but ours as well. Isaiah saw that moment, and he mourned, "Surely he hath borne our griefs, and carried our sorrows: yet we did esteem him stricken, smitten of God, and afflicted."[14]

Afflicted He was, my friends, as He prayed in the grim shadows of Gethsemane where not even the bosoms of His own disciples were available for His relief. With lonesomeness as His only companion and isolation as His only comrade, He stepped into the darkness of a woeful night, and because of His sorrowful weeping, He began to shed His blood even before a cruel hand was raised against Him.

Betrayed by one of His own, He is whisked away by a barbaric rabble. This, of course, was only by His submission, as they had just picked themselves up from the ground where they had been thrown by a flash of His divine power. Hassled and harassed all night long, insulted and abused by the ruthless mob, mockingly tried by a bloodthirsty tribunal, mercilessly tortured with the brutal whip, cowardly sentenced by a gutless governor, yet "he openeth not his mouth," even as "he is brought as a lamb to the slaughter."[15]

Picture the frightful scene, if you will, and recall that you, and not Christ, ought to have been the sorry subject of these horrors. Blood oozes from His head because a thorny crown penetrated His pores, and it was then driven deeper due to the blows from the soldiers' reed. Upon His back, there was more raw flesh to be seen than of His skin from the lashes of whips that feature particles of bone. Upon this marred back was placed the cross, which was modestly described as "rugged." And thus, He was compelled to journey to the place of His demise. But He cannot support it, as no one could, who had endured such a night and such a morning as He had endured. He fell several times beneath the unbearable load, until help was found at the hands of Simon of Cyrene.

After much struggling, straining, and further abuse from those sadistic soldiers, including the marring of His visage by the spittle of scoundrels as well as the taunts and insults from that horrid horde, they eventually reached Golgotha—the place of a skull—so called because of its chilling reputation; it was there that they crucified Him.

They crucified Him. This means that they stripped Him of His clothing and made Him lie down upon the cross, stretch His hands and feet to where they desired to have them, and pinned His limbs to the woodwork with crude and massive spikes. It means that they lifted the contraption with the Savior suspended on it and dashed it with violence[16] into its designated spot.

---

14   Isaiah 53:4
15   Isaiah 53:7
16   Ellen G. White, *The Desire of Ages* (Mountain View, CA: Pacific Press, 1898), 745.

Feel with Him, if you dare to, as the rusty nails ripped through His sensitive nerves, and He writhed in futile search of a posture that brings relief. Turn on the speakers of your soul and listen to the tumult of the red spot tragedy. Passersby revile Him with these words, "If thou be the Son of God, come down from the cross."[17] The spiritual leaders refuse to chide them, but signal their concurrence with mockery of their own: "He trusted in God; let him deliver him now." Even one of His

> *But for all the evil that it is, there is one characteristic of sin that I do not mind at all— sin is transferable!*

fellow candidates for death joins in the derision before His own voice drowns out all others with the plea: "My God, my God, why hast thou forsaken me?" Then He speaks with a solemn finality, "It is finished,"[18] at which point John tells us that He gives up the ghost.

As we ponder the happenings at "The Little Red Spot," we cannot help but ask ourselves what these things mean? Our purpose for going there is not accomplished until we wrestle with the reality of its implication for our lives. The sobering truth is: it was sin that took Him there, but it was not His sin, because He had none. It was your sin and mine.

"He was wounded for our transgressions, he was bruised for our iniquities: the chastisement of our peace was upon him; and with his stripes we are healed. All we like sheep have gone astray; we have turned every one to his own way; and the LORD hath laid on him the iniquity of us all."[19]

Now we look at what sin did to our Redeemer, and we cannot help but think that sin is the worst thing that has happened to this world. Sin is detestable. Sin is contemptible. Sin is unacceptable and totally objectionable. Sin in the sight of God is gruesome and grotesque. Sin is the culprit for societal degradation and spiritual depression. But for all the evil that it is, there is one characteristic of sin that I do not mind at all—sin is *transferable*! This doesn't mean that I can blame someone else for my wrongdoing, but it does mean that I can lay down my burden of guilt at the cross. You need not walk around with a weight of sin upon your back or upon your head because when Jesus shed His blood on your behalf, that sin was swept up in its flow. I really do not know how to explain this transaction. I will not even pretend to fully understand it. All I know is that when Jesus was arrested, we were acquitted; when He was bound, we were released; when He was condemned, we were issued liberty;

---

17   Matthew 27:40–46
18   John 19:30
19   Isaiah 53:5, 6

and when justice raised its arm against Him, we were covered in mercy and grace.

We have reason to rejoice because our sins are forgiven. We cannot but rejoice, for we have been set free. We can't help but be glad because the great Antitype—the Lamb of God—has taken away the sins of the world.[20]

Of course this is good news. This is the type of tidings that would drive sorrow from any sin-sick soul, but there is no one here who would forget that the price was high. There is no one here who would take this suffering lightly, and surely no one in the whole universe would take pleasure in it. Would you not agree?

Well, of course, the devil would be quite pleased. But apart from him and his sympathizers, no one else would have enjoyed this, true? Not so true. At least not according to Isaiah, for the prophet says, in verse 10 of chapter 53, that "it pleased the LORD to bruise Him."

What? It pleased the Lord to bruise Him, to put His own Son to grief? I find nothing in His bruising in which anyone should be pleased, let alone the compassionate Father, who is defined by John as love.[21] The devil's delight does not surprise me, for it was prophesied in Genesis that he would bruise Him, and with his fiendish self, he did take much pleasure in doing so, but not the Lord ... unless there was some sacred basis for this peculiar pleasure. And the truth is that there is. There is such a basis. That basis is *you*, and it is *me!*

The same text tells us how that is so. "He shall see His seed."

Let's pause for a moment here; we need to backpedal momentarily. This is something that you were told to remember. God had said to Satan, "I will put enmity between thee and the woman, and between thy seed and her Seed." And now Isaiah tells us that God was OK with the bruising because the Seed would see *His* seed.

Now, this is a line that gives me immense pleasure, because if I read correctly, it appears that the devil is being shown up. I know he is a smart fellow. I know he is a formidable foe. I would not dare to try to match him on my own. But my mind tells me that if Satan wanted to have the world to himself he should have left the Seed alone. He's a great psychologist and a wily strategist, but it is very obvious to me that Satan is a poor biologist! If that wasn't so, then the devil would have known that before a seed can spring forth and grow and multiply, it must first die. I don't know if he did not know the seed rule, or if he simply didn't know with whom he was dealing, but He unwisely put the Seed to death, and to make matters worse, he then buried Him in the earth.

Well, ladies and gentlemen, as they say, the rest is history. It didn't take too long for germination to begin. On Friday evening the Seed was planted. On the Sabbath

---

20   John 1:29
21   1 John 4:8

He rested, just as a natural seed goes through a period of dormancy until conditions are right for it for grow. Then on Sunday morning, with the conditions just right and the timing perfect and according to plan, He sprang forth from the earth and began a reproduction and multiplication process that has since then been unstoppable.

One Jesus was arrested. One Jesus was tried. One Jesus was sentenced. One Jesus was crucified. One Jesus was taken and buried in the grave. One Jesus waited there until the third day. The devil thought he had Him and that his foul mission was done. But little idea had he of that which was to come.

At the "red spot" his battle was only with Jesus, but after the resurrection, he had to contend with the Seed and *His* seed. He now had to try to control not just "this same Jesus,"[22] but the Jesus in His followers. He now had Jesus in the twelve disciples; there was Jesus in the 3,000 that were baptized at Pentecost; there was Jesus in the multitudes that took the message to their homelands; there was Jesus in the thousands who were convicted by their testimony; and there was Jesus in the countless who were daily added to the church as a result of the preaching of the gospel.

The devil got desperate and launched a furious seed-eradication campaign, but everywhere that one seed was snuffed out, countless others sprang up in its place. He has tried strategy after strategy, and he has repeatedly and miserably failed in all his attempts to halt the forward march of the truth.

It was this that made Jesus' suffering worth the pain He endured. He looked at the future and saw the fruit of His labor. As Isaiah aptly puts it, "He shall see the travail of his soul, and shall be satisfied." No wonder "it pleased the Lord to bruise him."

There is something else that Isaiah says that excites me greatly. In chapter 53:12, these words are found: "Therefore will I divide him a portion with the great, and he shall divide the spoil with the strong."

Like the great kings of old, He went to war. He emerged victorious and returned with the spoil of battle. I'm not sure if you might have interest in some red spot battle spoil, but I certainly do. Like a predaceous pirate, Satan attempted to hijack humanity, intending to rob it of its God-given bounties. But his operation was overthrown by One called the Lion of the tribe of Judah. The spoil has been bought back by the blood.

What spoil am I speaking of? That spoil is the joy that cheers you in the deepness of the night, the hope that helps you to look beyond, and the peace that consoles you when things go awry. It is the courage that propels you to strive for the mastery, the dignity that permits you to hold your head high, and the confidence that comes from being conscious that you are a conqueror. It encompasses the faith that compels

---

22   Acts 1:11

you to attempt the unthinkable, the identity that marks you as someone special, and the image of the Infinite in which you were created. It is the communion that brings you into the presence of God. This is what we lost through sin, which has now been brought back for us by the blood of the Lamb.

It is a very rich bounty, but it will be given to only those who truly desire it. The spoil will only be divided among the strong. It is not a bounty for weaklings and those who waver because it is only for the strong. If you are strong in your mind and spirit, in purpose and resolve, in the defense of righteousness and in resisting evil then you can take up *your* cross and follow the Lord; this cannot be accomplished in your strength, but "in the Lord, and in the power of his might,"[23] all this and more is yours. "Eye hath not seen, nor ear heard, neither have entered into the heart of man, the things which God hath prepared for them that love him."[24]

Now that Jesus has done what He has done, there remains no longer any pretext for feebleness and faintness. We now have access to the power that makes us strong. We can have power to defeat the devil, power to subdue sin, to triumph over temptation, and the power to live like Jesus. We have power to love the unlovable, live the unlivable, forgive the unforgivable, and to do the unthinkable. It's not an earthly power, but a heavenly power; it's not a human power, but a divine power; it's not a transient power, but a timeless power; and it's not a terrestrial power, but a celestial power. It's an amazing power, an attainable power, an available power, and an accessible power. It's a blood-bought power, a converting power, a dynamic power, and an energizing power. What a great power is this, paid for at Calvary, which transforms a wretch such as me into a son of the living God!

I am happy for Calvary today. I am grateful for the red spot. I am glad that God has so loved us, that He permitted Jesus to face Calvary's horrors, and that if we put our faith in Him, eternal life shall be ours. As I behold the cross of Calvary, I am humbled by the infinite love of God poured out upon this wayward race. What a view of the Father's character it gives us, so contrary to the false picture of a vengeful taskmaster God with a raised belt over His erring children, waiting to whip into submission any who might fall out of favor! It thrills me to have the privilege to reflect upon an act that captivates the interest of an entire universe. It humbles me to know that "God commendeth his love toward us, in that, while we were yet sinners, Christ died for us."[25]

By His hand we have been rescued, by His blood we have been redeemed, by His power we have been rejuvenated, and by His grace we are renewed. By His love we

---

23 Ephesians 6:10
24 1 Corinthians 2:9
25 Romans 5:8

have been ransomed, by His Spirit we are revived, by His Word we shall be resurrected, and at His appearing we shall be restored. Thank you, thank you, Jesus, for going to "The Little Red Spot!"

Mexico City, Mexico

"Life is a confusing jungle, but in this jungle we can find a path in Jesus."

Prologue

In October 2002 the youth department of the Inter-American Division of Seventh-day Adventists launched the inaugural Youth Satellite Evangelistic Campaign in Mexico City under the theme, *Viva Sin Temor* (Live Without Fear). This program, conceived and directed by IAD Youth Director Pastor Bernado Rodríquez, was planned against the backdrop of the multiple crises affecting our youth, and the ubiquitous apprehension resulting from the acts of terrorism that shocked the world on September 11, 2001.

The duration of the program was two weeks, and the presenters were youth representatives from about thirteen unions across Inter-America. I participated as the representative of the West Indies Union Conference.

My involvement in this event, mentioned briefly in previous and subsequent discourses in this series, was due to the recommendation of my close friend and colleague Steve Cornwall, then president of the ministerial association within the religion department of NCU, and Martin Hanna, then head of the department. Pastor Balvin Braham, then youth director of the West Indies Union Conference, accepted these recommendations and took on the responsibility for my orientation into the program. I am convinced, however, that my appointment ultimately came from a higher Source. There is no doubt in my mind that God intended for me to be part of this historic venture.

As a student, the price of participating in the *Viva Sin Temor* project was higher than I had anticipated. Preparation began with a one-week training program for the speakers and other personnel, which took place at the Montemorelos University in

Nuevo León, Mexico in February. Of course, this meant one week of absence in the middle of the semester, the implications of which were substantial.

In October I arrived in Mexico City two weeks prior to the program to facilitate a pre-campaign revival series at the Jardines de Morelos Church in Ecatepec. This again resulted in another extended absence from classes, a very trying semester, and my reluctant decision to turn down an invitation from United Student Movement sponsor, Noreen Daley, to run for the presidency of the student representative organization.

> *There are many people who are fearful and distressed by the difficulties that they face in their lives and the uncertainty and confusion that come with each day.*

However, as I would eventually come to see, God had His divine purpose in mind, and I had to wait until the dust settled to learn many of the lessons He had for me.

Looking back, I have to say that there was a singular movement of the Holy Spirit in the events in Mexico City. My own doubts about my call to the ministry of gospel proclamation were finally dismissed. Lifelong friendships were formed with a number of individuals. I also gained quite a bit of insight from my first real interaction with the Mexican people—an insight that would prompt me to move to that country four years later.

The privilege of communicating the gospel on such a grand and monumental stage had a dual effect upon me. There was, in the first place, an ineffable joy that I felt. And then, I was awfully humbled to have been so honored to be there, especially as I considered the humble circumstances of my own birth and upbringing—a thought which brought irrepressible tears of gratitude as I came to the end of the sermon.

My assigned subject was "The Sabbath: An Oasis for a Tired Heart." A transcript of that evening's discourse now follows.

The Message: An Oasis for a Tired Heart

"They went into Capernaum, and immediately on the Sabbath He entered the synagogue and taught … Now there was a man in their synagogue with an unclean spirit. And he cried out, saying, 'Let us alone. What have we to do with You, Jesus of Nazareth? Did You come to destroy us? I know who You are—the Holy One of God!' But Jesus rebuked him, saying, 'Be quiet, and come out of him.' And when the unclean spirit had convulsed him and cried out with a loud voice, he came out of him."
Mark 1:21–26, NKJV

Let me join in welcoming you to another session in this grand youth campaign here in Mexico City. I greet you with the warmth and love of the West Indies Union family. We are truly blessed to have another opportunity to study the Word of God and to listen to His voice as He speaks to our hearts.

I am very happy for this campaign, and I'm sure that those of you who are participating are also happy because it tells us about living without fear. The fact is that there are many people who are fearful and distressed by the difficulties that they face in their lives and the uncertainty and confusion that come with each day. But I thank God that you and I can live without fear because of the hope that is offered in His Word.

As I think about the pervasive panic in our world today, I am reminded of an encounter Jesus had during His ministry that, no doubt, drove fear into many of those who witnessed it. The story is found in Mark 1:21–26. "They went into Capernaum, and immediately on the Sabbath He entered the synagogue on the Sabbath and taught ... Now there was a man in their synagogue with an unclean spirit. And he cried out, saying, 'Let us alone. What have we to do with You, Jesus of Nazareth? Did You come to destroy us? I know who you are—the Holy One of God!' But Jesus rebuked him, saying, 'Be quiet, and come out of him.' And when the unclean spirit had convulsed him and cried out with a loud voice, he came out of him."

Looking at the man in this story, I could not help but see that there are many people in the world today who are not much different from him. They may not be possessed by a literal demon, but they are trapped. They are bound. They are enslaved. They are driven by a deviant, innate power that needs to be dispelled. It may be that tradition has them shackled. Some may be bound by prejudice. Others may be enslaved by misleading doctrines that conflict with the clear teaching of God's Word. But just as Jesus set that man free by casting the devil out of him, He desires to liberate us from all these shackles, so we can truly live without fear of uncertainty and deception.

We are told in the Bible that, "We wrestle not against flesh and blood, but against principalities, against powers, ... against spiritual wickedness in high places."[1] It is this power that is bent on creating ignorance, deception, vain traditions, and keeping people in confusion and willful disobedience. This power of darkness that possesses the human soul is bent on securing our allegiance in an effort to deny God the total allegiance that is due to Him. To this end, it engenders all kind of fear, causing people to worship God under duress and according to customs and traditions.

One of the amazing deceptions that this power imposes relates to the observance of the seventh day of the week, declared in the Bible to be the Sabbath of the Lord. It

---

1　　Ephesians 6:12

should not surprise us that the enemy would seek to assert his power by challenging one of God's Ten Commandments. We are warned that in these last days humankind would "think to change [God's] times and laws."[2] But I want to invite you to see the enlightening truth that the Bible teaches on this subject. And while preserving my utmost respect for Christians of all persuasions, I will proceed to share five essential biblical facts on this important subject.

In the first place, God *created* the Sabbath. We learn this from Genesis 2:1–3. "Thus the heavens and the earth were finished, and all the host of them. And on the seventh day God ended his work which he had made; and he rested on the seventh day … And God blessed the seventh day, and sanctified it: because that in it he had rested from all his work which God created and made." The Sabbath was the culmination of God's creation process. He created heaven and earth in six days, and on the seventh day, He created the Sabbath. It is in our best interest to give due regard to that which God has created. As Christians, we treat the environment with care because we recognize it is the handiwork of God. We regard human life with a sense of sacredness because it is God's creation. For the same reasons, we are required by God to observe the Sabbath, which He has specifically called our attention to by saying, "*Remember* the sabbath day, to keep it holy."[3] I am not sure how you see it, but I personally find it is unwise to forget something that God commands us to remember.

We cannot but treat the Sabbath with due reverence. After all, this is not one of man's fleeting and fatuous inventions. The God of the universe was the One who created the Sabbath. Mohammad did not create the Sabbath. Neither did Confucius. The Sabbath was not concocted by any of the great thinkers of the past. It did not originate in the minds of the apostles or the prophets. The early church fathers were not the founders of it. It did not come about by humankind's design. As far as I can see here, the Bible clearly states that it was created by God, blessed by God, made holy by God, set apart by God, and given to us by God. It is to remind us that God is Creator and that He is to be worshipped, respected, honored, and adored.

Now, not only did God create the Sabbath but He has also ordained a *specific day* of the week as the Sabbath. Genesis 2:2 says, "And on the seventh day God ended his work." Exodus 20:10 says, "The seventh day is the sabbath of the LORD." God does not leave us to speculate on this point or to elect our own Sabbath day. There are those who would advance the notion that this is a matter of personal preference, but the Bible is quite specific in speaking of the seventh day. There is a reason for this.

In an attempt to illustrate, I'd like to use a local example. I've observed that

2   Daniel 7:25
3   Exodus 20:8

many people here live in apartment buildings. Let us say that one Mr. Gonzalez has constructed an apartment building. There are seven apartments in the building, and he lives in apartment seven. All the apartments are similar in design, but there is something special about apartment seven: it is his place of residence. If you wish to visit with Mr. Gonzalez, you have no choice but to go to apartment seven. If you go to apartment one and ask for the owner, the tenant will tell you, "*Está en el apartamento numero siete.*" (He is in apartment number seven). If the neighbor is courteous like many of the Mexican people I've met, he will show you to the elevator or stairway so that you can be on your way to see Mr. Gonzalez in apartment seven. The same principle is true of God and the Sabbath. There are seven days in the week, and all seven were created by God. All seven have a twenty-four hour cycle. But there is only one day that God blessed, only one day in which God rested, only one day that He set apart as holy, and on this day, He requires all His children to lay aside their secular duties, fellowship with Him and with each other, and celebrate His act of creating the world. That makes the Sabbath unique, separate, and distinct from any other day.

Now, don't get me wrong. God is with us every day of the week. We can meet with Him on Sunday, Wednesday, Friday, or any other day. He expects us to worship Him on a daily basis, but he has set aside the seventh day, His "apartment seven," and has ordained that day as Sabbath.

For those who are confused about which day of week is the seventh day, the Bible and history provide us a superb clarification. In the book of Luke, we learn that the seventh day of the week is the day that follows the crucifixion and precedes the resurrection.[4] History tells us, and the annual Easter tradition bears it out, that our Lord was crucified on the sixth day, Friday, and rose on the first day, Sunday. The Sabbath, otherwise called Saturday, falls in the middle of those two.

Let me now mention briefly that the Sabbath was made for the *entire* human race. After God completed the creation of humanity on day six of creation week, He created the Sabbath and gave it to the representatives of the human race, Adam and Eve. The Sabbath was made before there was any named nationality. Before there were Mexicans, Venezuelans, or Jamaicans, there was the Sabbath. It was not a Jewish institution. All nations and races are of Adam's posterity. The Sabbath, given to the first couple by God, was thus, by extension, given to all their descendants. Jesus says, "The sabbath was made for man."[5] The Sabbath, in other words, was made for humankind. We have seen from the story we read earlier that Jesus kept the Sabbath, and we are taught that this was his lifestyle in Luke 4:16. If Jesus, our example, was careful to observe the Sabbath, and in His Holy Law enjoins us to

---

4   Luke 23:54; 24:1
5   Mark 2:27

remember its sacredness, we are left without doubt as to what He expects of those who profess to be His children.

The fourth point of emphasis is that the Sabbath will last *forever*. The Bible teaches that the Sabbath is perpetual. God Himself refers to it as "a perpetual covenant."[6] David tells us that "the works of his hands are verity and judgment; all his commandments are sure. They stand fast for ever and ever, and are done in truth and uprightness."[7] It is interesting that David should use the words "the works of his hands." Forty different authors wrote the Bible, but the Ten Commandments, including the one concerning the Sabbath, were written

> *Since all these other things that were made by God are still with us. Then the Sabbath is also still with us.*

by God Himself. The testimony of Moses concerning this is that "the tables were the work of God, and the writing was the writing of God, graven upon the tables."[8]

When God writes, humanity should take note. When God writes, humanity should read and seek to understand. When God writes, humanity should obey the written Word. When God writes, it is a call for special attention. The fact that God took time to write to us about the Sabbath indicates that it is very special to Him; it is not just something transient, but something that is as lasting as His nature. Jesus made this very clear when He issued the warning: "Think not that I am come to destroy the law, or the prophets: I am not come to destroy, but to fulfil. For verily I say unto you, Till heaven and earth pass, one jot or one tittle shall in no wise pass from the law, till all be fulfilled."[9]

There is another way to know that the Sabbath is still binding. The Sabbath was created in the same week when everything else was created. On day one God made light. Can we still see the light? Sure we can. On day two God made the heavens. Do you still see the heavens? Of course you do. On day three God made land and sea. I am still standing on the land, and I had to fly over the sea to get here! On day four God made the heavenly bodies. The sun still shines in all its glory. The moon has not refused to give her light. And the stars still twinkle in the twilight skies. On day five God made some of the animals. On my recent visit to the Chapultepec Zoo, I saw that there are some wonderful creatures there. On day six God made humankind. Do we still have people around? I would like to think so! On day seven God made the

---

6   Exodus 31:16
7   Psalm 111:7, 8
8   Exodus 32:16
9   Matthew 5:17, 18

Sabbath. Since all these other things that were made by God are still with us. Then the Sabbath is also still with us.

Not only is the Sabbath binding upon all people today, but it will be part of God's program in the new earth. God made the following promise through the prophet Isaiah, "For as the new heavens and the new earth, which I will make, shall remain before me, saith the LORD, so shall your seed and your name remain. And it shall come to pass, that from one new moon to another, and from one sabbath to another, shall all flesh come to worship before me, saith the LORD."[10] It is good to know that this oasis of rest and fellowship between God and His people is ours to enjoy not just for time, but for eternity; it is not just on earth, but in heaven.

The Sabbath is a fundamental pillar of God's creation that speaks to continuity in the universe. It speaks to the perpetuity of God. The Sabbath makes the point that there is a link between the future, the present, and the past. It speaks to the fact that God does not change, for He is the same yesterday, today, and forever. His Word stands fast, and we can count on Him, for He is a dependable God.

This brings us to the final point that I must highlight—the Sabbath represents *freedom* and *deliverance.* Considering this, I am reminded of our opening story. That man with the unclean spirit is a symbol of the human race. He stands as a representative of humanity in its lost and sinful state. When God created us, He created us in His image with a perfect and spotless character. However, we did not remain in that state for very long. Adam and Eve sinned by yielding to the temptation of the devil. By their choice, and now ours, we have become subject to satanic rule. The demon-possessed man is a classic example of what sin has done to humanity. But just as that man was set free by Jesus, you and I can be freed from sin. We can rest from the sorrows that plague us.

When the weekly Sabbath comes, we lay aside our secular activities to celebrate the creative act of God. But this weekly Sabbath also prefigures the day of deliverance, when we shall not only rest from the secular routine of life, but when we shall rest from the fears, sorrows, distress, and frustration of this earthly life. Indeed, the Sabbath is a symbol of deliverance. It is a token of ultimate freedom. It reminds us of the freedom that all God's people will enjoy when finally rescued from this world of sin and sorrow. I declare with joy that you may be free. We all may be free. And by keeping the Sabbath, we can begin to have a foretaste of that freedom even before it is fully realized.

The invitation of Christ to you and me is, "Come unto me, all ye that labour and are heavy laden, and I will give you rest."[11] He says, "I am the way, the truth, and the life."[12]

---

10   Isaiah 66:22, 23
11   Matthew 11:28
12   John 14:6

I remember the story of a young missionary in Africa who, one hot and tiresome day, lost his way in the middle of the jungle. He lumbered along until finally he came upon a group of natives. One of them volunteered to lead him back to the place where He was staying. With no path to walk on, they chopped their way through the dense bush until, exhausted, they sat down to rest. Overwhelmed again with the feeling of being lost, the missionary turned to the native and said, "Are you certain that we're going the right way? I don't see a path for us to walk on."

The native looked the missionary in the eye and said, "Sir, in this jungle there is no path. I am the path."

Life is a confusing jungle, but in this jungle we can find a path in Jesus. He leads us to find truth in the midst of our confusion. Jesus is the path that leads us to recognize that God created the Sabbath. He is the path that leads us to realize that the seventh day is the Sabbath. Jesus is the path that shows us that the Sabbath was made for the entire human race, and that it is perpetual by nature. He is the path that points us to the fact that the Sabbath represents freedom and deliverance.

Do you feel the need for guidance, for direction, for certainty? Come to Jesus. He is the Way. Are you seeking for true religion and a faith that is Bible-based? Come to Jesus. He is the Truth. Is it your desire to experience fulfillment and freedom in this world and the world to come? I invite you to come to Jesus. He alone is the Source of true life. If your heart is longing for rest and relief from the burdens you have been bearing, Jesus offers you the Sabbath—truly an oasis for a tired heart.

Newburgh, New York

"Don't just do something; stand there!"

Prologue

Almost immediately after my graduation from Northern Caribbean University in August 2003, I was assigned to the May Pen pastoral district for the commencement of my ministerial internship. I had the pleasure and the privilege of being understudy to Pastor Anthony Reid, with whom I enjoyed a dynamic working relationship during the time I served in his district.

Pastor Reid's innovativeness and keen eye for a capable leader allowed me to come in contact with a gentleman I have grown to admire and greatly respect— Howard Ottey. Ottey was in charge of the Adventist Youth Society at the May Pen Church when I met him, and we had numerous opportunities to chat, as it became a personal habit of mine to pass time with the youth of the church.

Sometime after leaving the district, I went back to May Pen to pay my friend a visit. It had been a while since we had communicated and there was someone he wanted me to meet. A pastor and friend of his for many years was conducting an evangelistic campaign in the community of Halse Hall. Ottey knew of my plans to take up an assignment in the United States within a few months. This was his way of ensuring that upon my arrival, there would be at least one familiar face that I could call upon. This is how I first met Pastor Trevor Stewart.

Trevor was the pastor of the Newburgh and Beacon Light Seventh-day Adventist Churches in New York. He had roots in Kingston and returned to Jamaica from time to time to run evangelistic series. On the night of our meeting, two things impressed me about him: his natural gift as a preacher of the gospel and his humble and engaging demeanor when we were introduced.

Not long after arriving at my post in New Hampshire, I set out to find my new friend, and he did not hesitate to put me to work. Before the end of our first conversation, I was booked for a speaking appointment at the Newburgh Church. This was followed by another visit, and yet another, and the ties of friendship rapidly extended from the pastor to this affable and gracious group of worshippers.

There were a number of individuals at this church who made it a point of duty to ensure that I always felt welcome, and the pleasant memories I have of Newburgh are largely owed to them. My reluctance to mention them all by name is only due to the fact that I have not obtained their consent to do so by this medium. But I cannot help but pay tribute to first elder Floyd Sam and his family, whose deep interest and affection remain with me even now.

It might have been on my second or third visit that I preached this sermon. The church was in low spirits because of the illness of its shepherd and my friend. We needed a word that was relevant to the crisis, and God did not fail to supply it. Through David, a man to whom grief was no stranger, and whose name is already a familiar sight in this series, yet another message was issued to remind the hearers that God is still tuned in to our cries, even if they come from the depths of the horrible pit.

The Message: Horrible Pits and New Songs

"I waited patiently for the Lord; and he inclined unto me, and heard my cry. He brought me up also out of an horrible pit, out of the miry clay, and set my feet upon a rock, and established my goings. And he hath put a new song in my mouth, even praise unto our God: many shall see it, and fear, and shall trust in the Lord." Psalm 40:1–3

We have before us today a most inspiring testimony from one who clearly understands what it means to walk with God. His testimony is even more intriguing when we observe that this writer is also acquainted with the bitterness of life *without* God. He, therefore, does not speak in abstract terms of his experiences because this is someone who is familiar with life's nights as well as its mornings. It is for these reasons that I bring you this message in confidence, for when David speaks, it is always a word that is well-founded. His life is his classroom, and his relationship with God is the textbook from which he takes these lessons that it is our privilege to review.

In the selected passage, he supplies us with a statement that highlights three stations in his encounter with God: the horrible pit, the rock, and the new song. Before drawing your attention to these, however, let us look at what these verses reveal about their author.

I find, first of all, that here is someone who believes in the power of *praise*. In these verses he declares the potency of praise not just as a means of demonstrating one's appreciation of God but also as a method of testifying to others about Him. But in this passage we also find that David understands the priority of *prayer*. There seems to be, in the psyche of the psalmist, a precedence of prayer over praise in the Christian experience.

> *Our praise takes on a new relevance and efficacy when it is issued from lips that commune consistently with Christ.*

If we look closely, it will become clear to us that David received his song only after he had cried unto the Lord and waited patiently for His reply. I believe that this shepherd king intended for us to know that we cannot truly praise God until we learn how to pray. It is obvious that his praise life depended heavily upon his prayer life. This is how it is with the connected Christian. Our praise takes on a new relevance and efficacy when it is issued from lips that commune consistently with Christ.

It is by prayer that we get to know Him. It is by prayer that we connect our hearts with His. It is by prayer that we show how much we love Him and how much we cannot live without Him. It is in prayer that we bring to bear the full force of our faith and obtain access to the bounties of His grace.

Praise without a prayer foundation amounts to nothing but an irrelevant religious ritual. It is as strange as shouting accolades to someone you do not know. Think of someone who you hardly ever talk to, or someone you know at best as a casual acquaintance. Then think of yourself making much of that person in a public place by telling him or her how much he or she means to you. You go on about how you appreciate him or her and that your thoughts revolve around him or her. You can serenade him or her with lines that tell him or her that he or she is the reason for which you live. But you see where this is going—it is a blatant lie, and many such lies are told on weekends in places of worship around the world.

If you want to truly praise Him, have a chat with Him before searching for your song. If you want to truly praise Him, make some changes and put the prayer meeting on your agenda. If you intend to praise Him, make sure He can acknowledge it as coming from a friend. If you do not, the sad reality is that it will mean nothing to Him.

That friendship will not come about without prayer, and by "prayer" I do not mean routinely talking at God. There was nothing ordinary about David's prayer. It called for some waiting, and it required some weeping. This was not a verbose heaven-directed recitation. From what I perceive, his plot was not to impress people with his power-packed praying prowess. I do not even think anyone was around to hear him praying. I believe we only know about it because he placed it in our text. It might not have been eloquent, but it was effective. It might not have been impressive, but it was heartfelt. It might not have been public, but it was surely persistent; and when his heart was full, his tears became the words that his lips could no longer utter. It is no wonder that his praise was so mighty. It was a praise that proceeded out of an importunate soul.

If we learn the lesson well, we shall soon discover that we can praise God mightily in public only when we pray to Him persistently in private. There are people in this place today who know to what I am referring. There is someone in here listening who can identify with David. Someone knows what it is like to be bogged down by a burden, and you understand what crying unto the Lord means. You did not merely ask, but you begged. You pleaded. You did not just seek, but you pursued. You persisted. You did not just knock, you pushed against the door until your energy left you, and all your strength was spent. You know very well where David is coming from not merely because you read it in the Book, but because you have been there yourself.

> *One thing is clear: the manner of his entry had no bearing upon the certainty of his exit …*

David does not share with us the subject of his prayer. All he gives us is this meaningful metaphor: he was in a *horrible pit.* He does not give us specifics, and that is just as well, for there are a great number of tragedies that he endured during the course of his life that would make a perfect match with this description. We are not sure if he spoke of his mistreatment by his brothers when he proposed to challenge that apostate Philistine, or his anguish when hunted by Saul for his life. We do not know if this pit refers to his moral fall with Bathsheba, or to the death of the child they conceived. It is not clear whether it was the crisis with his son, Amnon, or the tragedy of the loss of his beloved Absalom. But whatever it was, it haunted his soul so much that he was obliged to cry out to the Lord.

As to how David got into the pit, we are not told even this. We are ignorant as to whether he was thrown down into it unwittingly, or if, by his own actions, he dug his own pit and later fell inside it, as many of us often do. One thing is clear: the manner of his entry had no bearing upon the certainty of his exit, for he called upon the Lord with a sincere and contrite heart. When David knocked on heaven's door, he was not handed a personal history questionnaire to specify whether it was by his fault or that of another that he came to occupy the horrible pit. All he tells us is that he cried. All he tells us is that he waited and that the Lord heard him.

This gives me hope because whereas I was always sure the Lord would deliver me from my enemies, I never had much confidence that He would deliver me from myself. But now that David has spoken, my doubts have finally dissipated. There are those of you who have struggled with this matter for years. You know that it was you who put you in the pit where you find yourself. And for years the devil told you that there is no coming out. This amounts to falsehood and a diabolic deception of the lowest sort. Not only does God forgive the sinner who sins against another but His grace also extends even to the sinner who sins against himself.

As to the pits we encounter in our sojourn here, they are more than can be mentioned. You may not be in a horrible pit right now, but that is because you have either just come out of one or your pit awaits you along your path. One thing is sure: at some point in our walk through this life, we will find ourselves stranded in the mire of a horrible pit. And the fact that you have already traversed one does not mean that you may not have to negotiate another.

There are pits of financial misery. There are pits of occupational unrest. There are pits of mental perplexity. There are pits of parental distress. There are pits of moral indiscretion. There are pits of emotional collapse. There are pits of social tension. There are pits of spiritual estrangement.

I do not know what pit you might find yourself in. All I know is that you do not have to stay there forever. David made a transition, and so can you. The important thing is that you avoid getting comfortable in the pit. The key issue is that you do not ever accept the pit life as an unchangeable reality. You must tell yourself, "This is not me. This is not God's plan for my life. There is more to me than the present circumstances indicate. I may be in a pit now, but not for long. I may not be able to get myself out, but I know who can. I will cry to God, and I know He will hear my cry." As long as you do that, you can be sure that a positive change is on the way for you.

That change did come for David, and this is how he reports it, "He brought me up also out of an horrible pit, out of the miry clay, and set my feet upon a rock, and established my goings."

Look and learn of the wonderful way in which God works. He took David from an undesirable place and put him in the most desirable place. He removed him from a place where he pined in his solitude and put him in a place where he was in full view of others. He took him out a place of distress and misery and put him in a place of rapture and peace.

God is not just interested in taking us from the worst. He is totally committed to taking us to the best. There is no more fitting replacement for the horrible pit than the solid Rock. In the pit he had no direction. In the pit he had no purpose. In the pit he had no self-worth. In the pit he had no peace. In the pit he had no admirers. In the pit he had no friends. In the pit he had no fan club. In the pit he had no appeal. But the story remarkably changed when he was relocated to the rock.

When on the rock, he had a sure foundation. When on the rock, he obtained a sense of direction. When on the rock, he found a reason for living and his existence took on new meaning.

I might as well tell you that life cannot ever be better than when you are standing upon the solid Rock Christ Jesus. First of all, it is unwise to stand anywhere else. The blessed hymn writer put it this way, "On Christ, the solid Rock, I stand; all other ground is sinking sand."

When Jesus was looking for a foundation for His church, He was looking for the base on which to plant the first stone—a foundation that would withstand the assaults of hell. It had to be one that would weather all the spiritual storms into which it would be hurled. I imagine He said to Himself, "I am not going to build my church upon wisdom. I will not build it upon wealth. I will not lay the foundations upon intellect. Neither will I build it upon strength. I will build my church upon the surest foundation on which anything can be built. I will build my church upon 'this rock'[1]—Myself, for only then can I be sure that hell will not prevail against it."

I believe that this placing of David upon the rock has a dual significance. It shows, first of all, what a great difference it makes to have Christ as our foundation. But I believe there might be a subtle reference here to the indispensability of the church in the life of the believer and in his or her spiritual well-being. I feel that being on the Rock is synonymous with being in the church. You cannot be on the Rock and not in the church because the church is built upon the Rock.

I thought I would mention this because there are some folk who choose to remain in the pit of sin because they do not wish to associate with some of those who are on the Rock! The church has a sure foundation, but this does not mean that it is perfect. The Builder is working on the structure even now. So regardless of the imperfections, get on the Rock! Regardless of the hitches and glitches, get on the Rock! It is much better and safer and makes more sense than remaining in the horrible pit anyway.

The solution to the crisis of the horrible pit is Jesus, the Rock of Ages. If the crisis is financial, He is the owner of the world's resources. If the crisis is occupational, He's the boss of all employers. If the crisis is mental, there is no greater psychologist than He. If the crisis is parental, He is the fountain of wisdom. If the crisis is moral, He is our advocate. If the crisis is social, He is the great peacemaker. If the crisis is spiritual, He is our Redeemer. And if the crisis is physical illness, I should remind you that He is our balm in Gilead and our Great Physician.

No matter what your pit is, if you pray earnestly enough, if you wait patiently enough, not only will your Rescuer incline toward you and hear you but He will also

---

1   Matthew 16:18

reach down into the miry clay, lift you out of that ditch, place you upon His own shoulder, and take you in a new direction. I would happily exchange the quagmire of the horrible pit for a divine "jockey ride" any day. If you ask me what my preference is, I would tell you that I would rather be on Jesus' shoulders!

I want to now bring you to the best part of David's story. So far he has told us that he was in a horrible pit. He has told us that he called upon the Lord. He has told us that he waited patiently. He has told us that his prayer was answered, and that he was given a change of location from the pit to the rock. But that is only a part of the story. David's testimony is not complete. Pay attention: "And he hath put a new song in my mouth, even praise unto our God."

A new song! David says the Lord gave him a *new* song when He took him out of the pit, which is to say, that David already knew something about singing even before he came out of the pit. If he was given a new song, it means that in the pit he was singing an *old* song. Yes, he was singing while he was down there! His was a song of deepening depression and frightening fear. It was a song of sickening solitude and gut-wrenching guilt. It was a song of dreadful disillusionment and haunting hopelessness and maddening misery. His songs did not calm

> *You need not say to someone, "I am standing on the Rock." If he can hear your song, he will know where your feet are.*

him while he was in the pit. His symphonies were not soothing to the soul while in the pit. His music compounded his misery, for these were songs that told the tale of his terror while he was forced to grapple with the realities of the horrible pit lifestyle.

But when he was brought out, a new song was given to him. It was not a song of despair, but a song of hope. It was not a song of sorrow. It was a song of joy. It was not a song about the night. It was a song about the morning. It was not a song about his distress. It was a song about his deliverance.

Let me make the point that we have all been singing something throughout our lives, and the song we sing depends upon the spot on which we stand. In the pit we sing the songs of the pit. But on the rock we sing a different tune. It is your song that tells your story. You need not say to someone, "I am standing on the Rock." If he can hear your song, he will know where your feet are. If you are like David, you will find that God will change not just your location but He will also change your vocation: from pining in the pit to rejoicing on the rock. You will go from wasting in distress to walking in delight because He does not only change your circumstance; He changes your song.

The liar in the pit becomes an advocate of truth on the Rock. The thief in the pit becomes a practitioner of honesty on the Rock. The profane in the pit becomes a symbol of purity on the Rock. The promiscuous in the pit becomes an example of chastity on the Rock.

As for me, I want to testify that my song has changed not just symbolically but also literally. In the pit I sang an old song: "Unbreak my heart. Say you love me again."[2] But now I sing a new song: "Search me, O God, and know my heart today."[3] In the pit I used to sing an old song: "Speechless, speechless, that's how you make me feel."[4] But now I sing a new song: "Oh for a thousand tongues to sing my great Redeemer's praise."[5] In the pit I sang an old song: "I found love on a two way street and lost it on a lonely highway."[6] But I have a new song now: "The love of God is greater far than tongue or pen can ever tell. It goes beyond the highest star and reaches to the lowest hell.... Oh, love of God how rich and pure, how measureless and strong. It shall forevermore endure the saints and angels' song."[7]

Today, you too can sing a new song. If you have the confidence to cry out to the Creator, the patience to persevere with your plea, the faith to fix your focus upon the Father, and the hope to hang on to heaven, you shall soon find yourself rising from the depths of the dungeon. And as you rise, you will hear a musical melody ringing from your own lips: "Forgetting those things which are behind, and reaching forth unto those things which are before, I press toward the mark for the prize of the high calling of God in Christ Jesus."[8]

I say to you, press onwards. Press upwards. And don't stop pressing; don't stop pushing; don't stop praying; don't stop pleading; don't stop prompting; and don't stop plowing, until the walls of the horrible pit give way, and you stand upon the solid Rock of victory. And when you get up on the Rock, I want you to do something: stand there!

Now I know this might sound unconventional because you are accustomed to being told, "Don't just stand there, do something." But you have already done all you can. You have labored all your life. You have watched. You have worked. You have prodded, and you have prayed. So when you get up on that Rock, only this once, don't just do something, stand there!

Stand there, where no human hand can displace you. Stand there, where no human word can discredit you. Stand there, where no human thought can disorient you. Stand there, where no human plot can dislodge you. Stand there, where no

2　　Toni Braxton, "Unbreak My Heart"
3　　J. Edwin Orr, "Search Me, O God"
4　　Michael Jackson, "Speechless"
5　　Charles Wesley, "O for a Thousand Tongues to Sing"
6　　Sylvia Robinson and Bert Keyes, "Love on a Two-Way Street"
7　　Frederick Lehman, "The Love of God"
8　　Philippians 3:13, 14

human hate can dishearten you. Stand there, where no human praise can distract you. "Stand still, and see the salvation of the LORD."[9]

"Take unto you the whole armour of God, that ye may be able to withstand in the evil day, *and having done all, to stand.*"[10]

You do not have to give a victory speech. Just stand on the Rock. And David prophesies that while you are there standing, something will begin to happen: "Many shall see it, and fear, and shall trust in the LORD."

They will not just hear your new song; they will see it! Its notes will be printed all over your countenance. Its words will be written all over your visage. Its lines will be traced across your face. Its chords will be engraved all over your being.

Your life will be a testimony. Your song will be a witness. Your victory will be an example. Your journey will become a parable. Your experience will be a marvel. Your story will be a sign. Your deliverance will be the evidence that yours is a merciful God.

---

9   Exodus 14:13
10   Ephesians 6:13, emphasis added

Montemorelos, Mexico

"Yet the lie itself bothers me much less than the willingness of good people to believe it."

Prologue

The thirty-third chapter of the book of Ezekiel brings into focus an aspect of the work of the professed servant of God that is often ignored and greatly despised by a growing number of modern preachers. Inasmuch as the majority of congregants would rather listen to that which is agreeable—a kind of pseudo gospel rather than the unadulterated truth—many preachers today, in the quest to increase or to maintain their popularity, tend to stay away from such subjects as would arouse opposition or the semblance of any controversy. But the question may be asked: can any preacher be considered faithful if his premise for preaching always matches the particular preferences of his parishioners? Is it not the preacher's first duty to proclaim the Word of God as it is written, without any consideration for the approbation of fellow human beings?

This book has been written to inspire souls who have somehow found themselves engulfed in the darkness of a midnight tragedy. It speaks to those who have become acquainted with the horrible pit and are seeking a way out of it. It encourages the one who has been smitten with that leprous malady known to us as sin. But there is also a place in this volume for a watchman's warning word. I understand from the heavenly mandate that when the watchman sees the enemy approaching the city entrusted to his care then he has a duty to fulfill—a duty that does not by any means involve silence or complacency. He must stand in his lot. He must lift up his voice. He must make known the stark reality that death lies at the door. He must stir the people to action. He cannot be slothful or he must bear the bloody burden of the souls he failed to warn. Perhaps the darkest night is when the armies of the father of lies bear down upon Zion, and the weapons of false doctrine are launched against the city of the living God.

Every member of the true body of Christ has a solemn Christian duty to hold accountable those who bear the weighty responsibility of providing spiritual guidance to the people of God. In the special context of our times, it is a most grievous sin against God and against humanity to remain in silence while false ideas are being taught and Bible truth is being distorted. God will not regard as innocent those who refuse to take a stand against error simply because of a cowardly desire to avoid reproach or opposition.

It is even a greater sin to claim that certain controverted points of doctrine are not of such great importance as to be challenged and that to question certain spurious teachings is to engage in vain disputes, to show contempt for authority, or to needlessly attack others who have a different point of view. The claim is *false* that those who seek to distinguish truth from error are the instigators of dissent and confusion. On the contrary, those who bring about confusion are those who corrupt the truth of God by introducing error, and it is the duty of the child of God to denounce the lie and uphold only that which the Bible supports.

How dare anyone assert that that which undermines God's truth is non-essential or trivial? Who is so audacious as to affirm that the teaching of heresy is inconsequential and not worth the scrutiny and opposition of every child of God? When the Bible warns that souls will be lost because they have been made drunk with false concepts about God and the doctrines of His Holy Word, who would have the temerity to declare that this is but a light matter? When the Almighty has spoken and declared that the world is in danger when it has imbibed the deadly wine of Babylon and is therefore ripe and ready for the last plagues, who would dare to claim that it is not a cause for alarm that some should taste but a few drops of the lethal wine?

With these matters in mind, the reader is now invited to contemplate a most vital subject that is pertinent to our present spiritual experience—that of the incarnation of the Savior. The quietude of northern Mexico afforded me ample opportunity to reflect and research this subject deeply in the time I sojourned there. So urgent do I consider this matter that I feel obliged to include it in this collection without ever having given this discourse in a live presentation. The reader will therefore readily observe a slight variance in the nature and scope of the present chapter.

May the Word again come alive to each heart, and may truth shine mightily and gloriously from the inspired pages, so that the armies of falsehood may be utterly confounded and thoroughly vanquished, and Christ may crush Satan under His feet yet again.

The Message: The Word Made Flesh

"Beloved, believe not every spirit, but try the spirits whether they are of God: because many false prophets are gone out into the world. Hereby know ye the Spirit of God: Every spirit that confesseth that Jesus Christ is come in the flesh is of God: And every spirit that confesseth not that Jesus Christ is come in the flesh is not of God: and this is that spirit of antichrist, whereof ye have heard that it should come; and even now already is it in the world."1 John 4:1–3

John, that disciple who leaned on Jesus' breast—the Beloved, the revelator, the last apostle to survive the chosen twelve who walked with the incarnate Savior on His brief sojourn here—speaks to us of his dear Master in his gospel, in his three epistles, and in Revelation. He speaks with assurance and with precision, as one who was acquainted with our Redeemer more than any of his contemporaries. Indeed, there is an air of sublime and holy confidence in his assertions concerning Christ, as we would expect from one who has walked side by side with Jesus, familiar with the ups and downs of His earthly experience. This John, the former "son of thunder," now molded, humbled, and refined by the beauty of his Lord's character, takes pen to hand and sets out to introduce his Lord to the world. He does not begin by the seaside with the fishing boats and the unanticipated and irresistible invitation to "follow Me." He does not start with the first miracle that announced to Palestine that Someone special had arrived. No! He goes back to the beginning, and to the beginning he draws us—where the Word was, and where "the Word was with God" and where "the Word was God."[1] Ah! Note carefully, he does not say, "the Word was *a god*," as certain books[2] passed off as "bibles" say today. Not at all! The Word, Jesus his Lord, on whose breast he leaned, "was God!" (Now that is some place to lay your head!)

In no uncertain terms, John lays down the divinity of Jesus Christ. There is no room in his writings for that abysmal heresy of the Arian variety, which denies the eternal co-existence of Christ with the Father. But His language is unmistakable, and with equal assurance, the apostle goes on to introduce the subject with which we are concerned today—the humanity of Christ. He says, "And the Word was made flesh, and dwelt among us."[3] So this John, the beloved disciple of Jesus our Lord, declares *without reservation* both the divinity as well as the humanity of Christ.

Now when the disciple John tells us that "the Word was made flesh," there is a natural question that automatically arises in the analytical and careful mind. That

---

1   John 1:1
2   The New World Translation of the Bible
3   John 1:14

question is: into what kind of flesh was the Word made? What kind of flesh did the Savior assume in His incarnation? In other words, what kind of human nature did Jesus have while He walked as a man upon this earth? There are only two possibilities before us. The first is the nature of Adam in his sinless state in the Garden of Eden. The second is the nature of humankind after the entrance of sin into our world. When Christ, the Word, was made flesh, was He made in the flesh of sinless Adam or did He take the human nature of every child of Adam?

God be praised that we are not left to conjecture upon this vital point of Christian faith. That it is a vital point we know from this inspired statement: "The humanity of the Son of God is everything to us. It is the golden chain that binds our souls to Christ, and through Christ to God. This is to be our study."[4] If "the humanity of the Son of God is everything to us" and "is to be our study," then we may forthwith dispose of any proposition or claim that the matter is too mysterious to be understood. We need to follow with diligence the precious rays of light that God has shed on the subject. I say this while recognizing that not everything that has to do with the incarnation of the Savior has been opened to human understanding, but "those things which are revealed belong unto us and to our children."[5] For our own sakes then, and for our children, we go to that which the inspired writings reveal.

Paul's very first words in his first epistle in the New Testament include a bold statement about the human nature of Christ. It is part of the foundation upon which he builds his theology. It seems as though "the humanity of the Son of God" was "everything to" the apostle Paul. I am led to this conclusion because of the following observation: this man of God, called to be the chief communicator of the gospel of Christ to the world in his day, has not even completed the first introductory sentence of his epistle to the Romans before presenting the doctrine of the human nature of Christ! Indeed, it is the very first doctrinal point that he makes in the book of Romans, for he says, "Concerning his Son Jesus Christ our Lord, which was made of the seed of David according to the flesh."[6] Surely the expression "thou Son of David"[7] takes on a new and richer and more personal meaning when we consider that Jesus "was made of the seed of David according to the flesh."

> *Thank God that fallen humanity has a Savior who understands its infirmities through His personal experience.*

---

4   Ellen G. White, "Search the Scriptures," *The Youth's Instructor,* October 13, 1898.
5   Deuteronomy 29:29
6   Romans 1:3
7   Luke 18:38

Paul, expanding some more on this very point a little further on in his letter to the Romans, asserts the following: "For what the law could not do, in that it was weak through the flesh, God sending his own Son in the likeness of sinful flesh, and for sin, condemned sin in the flesh."[8] It is evident that if God sent His Son "in the likeness of sinful flesh," then He could not have sent Him in the likeness of sinless flesh, such as that of Adam before the fall! And if this (the incarnation) was done to condemn sin in the flesh, then it is His very coming in sinful flesh which made such condemnation possible. Thank God that fallen humanity has a Savior who understands its infirmities through His personal experience, and that through this experience, He has been able to carve out a pathway of victory into which each one may confidently enter by the bounties of His matchless grace.

It is this same line of coherent thought that the apostle Paul carries over into the book of Hebrews[9] where, as John does, he first establishes the divinity of Christ (in chapter one) and goes on to set forth Christ's humanity (in chapter two). Here, as in Romans 8:3, he explains not just the fact that Christ partook of the fallen human nature of "the seed of Abraham," but he goes further to address us upon the subject of *why* this choice was necessary. Listen here: "Forasmuch then as the children are partakers of flesh and blood, he also himself likewise took part of *the same*; that through death he might destroy him that had the power of death, that is, the devil." [10]

When Paul says in Romans 8:3 that Christ came to earth "in the likeness of sinful flesh," he means just that. We have no right to defiantly postulate that he meant to say the opposite of what he actually said. Some creative minds would try to convince us that this word "likeness" (Greek: *homoiōma*), when analysed in the original, can be interpreted to mean not "like," as it obviously says, but rather "unlike!" Now this, I must say, is creative—and deceptive—theology at its very best. Beware of it, my dear friends. What Paul states in Romans he restates in Hebrews. What kind of flesh did Jesus take? "The same" as all the children of Abraham.

This passage in Hebrews is another clear statement from the Word of God on the subject of Jesus' human nature. The reasons for this reality are so vividly delineated that confusion and misunderstanding are totally impossible. Says the apostle: "For verily he took not on him the nature of angels; but he took on him the seed of

---

8   Romans 8:3
9   Despite the divisive disputes that abound today concerning the authorship of the book of Hebrews, the attentive reader of the Spirit of Prophecy writings will find an abundance of evidence there to confirm that the author was indeed Paul. Examples of such evidence may be found in: *The Spirit of Prophecy*, vol. 4, page 256, *Lift Him Up*, page 372, and *The Great Controversy*, page 512. The fact that many theologians, even while knowing these references, continue to assert that no one knows who authored the book of Hebrews only serves to give credence to the inspired prediction that the last deception of Satan will be to make void the testimonies of the Spirit of God.
10   Hebrews 2:14, emphasis added

Abraham."[11] A translation into English of this verse as given in the Spanish Reina Valera Gómez Bible reads thus: "For surely he did not take for himself the nature of the angels, but he took that of the seed of Abraham." And why did He take such a nature? The answer is emphatic and precise: "Wherefore in all things it behoved him to be made like unto his brethren, that he might be a merciful and faithful high priest in things pertaining to God, to make reconciliation for the sins of the people. For in that he himself hath suffered being tempted, he is able to succour them that are tempted."[12]

If the authoritative Word of God says that it "behoved" Christ "to be made like His brethren," not half-way, but "in all things," who has the authority to assert that in His human nature He was never fully like us, but took the nature of angels, or, for that matter, the sinless nature of Adam before the fall? Well, no one has such authority, but someone thinks he has the authority to undermine the Word of God in so pivotal a subject. And as we shall see in a little while, this is none other than antichrist himself!

So far we have gathered from the Word of God several key points regarding our subject. We have seen that Jesus assumed sinful flesh and condemned sin in that flesh. He condemned sin in the only way that sin could be condemned—by taking fallen nature upon Himself and in that nature living a sinless life. He lived a sinless life in fallen flesh by walking after the Spirit and not after the (fallen) flesh. Because of this amazing victory, which leaves Satan in the unenviable refuse pile of embarrassment and defeat, Christ makes it possible for human beings to do the same. The incarnation and holy life of the Redeemer, along with His death and present intercessory work, means that human beings have no excuse for sin, though encumbered by a fallen nature. All this comprises a priceless and pressing truth—the very heart of the everlasting gospel—which Satan and his minions would be loathe to confess and would do their very best to conceal or deny.

It is very important that we understand that when the Bible says Jesus was made "in the likeness of sinful flesh," or that He took the nature of the "seed of Abraham," or even that He was made "to be sin for us," it does not mean to say He was a sinner. William Wirth offers the following clarification: "Just as the brazen serpent was a Deliverer to the Israelites in the likeness of the fiery serpent that destroyed, so Christ came as the Saviour of the world in the likeness of men that sin. Just as the brazen serpent, though in the form of a fiery serpent, was without venom, so Jesus, though in the form of sinful man, was without sin."[13]

We have been duly warned: "Be careful, exceedingly careful as to how you dwell

---

11   Hebrews 2:16
12   Hebrews 2:17, 18
13   William Wirth, *Signs of the Times*, April 22, 1930, 6.

upon the human nature of Christ. Do not set Him before the people as a man with the propensities of sin.... He took upon Himself human nature, and was tempted in all points as human nature is tempted.... But not for one moment was there in Him an evil propensity."[14]

While we uphold the biblical testimony that our Lord fully identified with us, we must never draw into doubt the absolute purity of His character. This is a matter that we all must understand. Perhaps nowhere is this truth more eloquently stated than in the following pronouncement by the messenger of the Lord: "In taking upon Himself man's nature in its fallen condition, Christ did not in the least participate in its sin.... Could Satan in the least particular have tempted Christ to sin, he would have bruised the Saviour's head. As it was, he could only touch His heel.... We should have no misgivings in regard to the perfect sinlessness of the human nature of Christ.... This holy Substitute is able to save to the uttermost; for He presented to the wondering universe a perfect and complete humility in His human character, and perfect obedience to all the requirements of God."[15] Again, we are told: "Christ took our nature, fallen but not corrupted, and would not be corrupted unless He received the words of Satan in place of the words of God."[16]

The Lord said of Himself, "The prince of this world cometh, and hath nothing in me."[17] This means that He never once yielded to the devil's temptation. The preceding quotation is unequivocally clear that the Redeemer never participated in sin, which is the transgression of the law, according to the Scriptures. We are called upon to follow His sinless example, not by trusting in our own merits, but by submitting to the transforming power of the grace of God. This becomes clearer as soon as we understand a basic truth about the nature of sin. The sinfulness of humanity is found, not in the fallen nature that we possess, but in the wrong employment of the *will*. No one is condemned by God because of the weakened constitution of human nature, as this is only the *result* of Adam's fall.

> *When Paul states that "whatsoever is not of faith is sin," he means that whatever is not of faith violates the principles of the law of God.*

---

14 Ellen G. White, *The SDA Bible Commentary,* vol. 5 (Washington D.C.: Review and Herald Publishing Association, 1956), 1128. The *Merriam-Webster's Collegiate Dictionary, 13th edition,* defines "propensity" as "a strong natural tendency to do something."

15 Ellen G. White, Selected Messages, book 1, (Washington D.C.: Review and Herald Publishing Association, 1958), 256.

16 Ellen G. White, *Manuscript Releases*, vol. 16 (Silver Spring, MD: Ellen G. White Estate, 1990), 182, 183.

17 John 14:30

No one is condemned by God because of an act committed by an ancestor. Each one bears the consequences of his or her choices. As Paul explains, sin is the result of yielding to the tempter, but not even Satan, with all his power to tempt and annoy, can force the weakest soul to sin, unless that soul lets go of God. "Know ye not, that to whom ye yield yourselves servants to obey, his servants ye are to whom ye obey; whether of sin unto death, or of obedience unto righteousness?"[18]

For those who would argue for a Christology other than that presented in the Bible, a redefinition of sin has become necessary. But again, the inspired Testimonies are a bulwark against all such fanciful speculations and doctrines of humankind. The messenger of God says to us, "Our only definition of sin is that given in the word of God; it is 'the transgression of the law.' "[19] If this is so, then whatever else the Bible tells us about sin must not be considered as an alternative definition, thus making the Bible appear to contradict itself, but must rather be understood in the context of this all-encompassing definition. For example, when Paul states that "whatsoever is not of faith is sin,"[20] he means that whatever is not of faith violates the principles of the law of God.

The following statement is also helpful in bringing us to a right understanding of the nature of sin: "But while Satan can solicit, he cannot compel to sin.... The tempter can never compel us to do evil.... The *will* must consent."[21] So human beings are not guilty before God merely for possessing a fallen nature, for that fallen nature—that sinful flesh—cannot sin of its own accord nor is it guilty of sin merely for the sake of being fallen flesh. We are told that "the flesh of itself cannot act contrary to the will of God."[22] Even our fallen flesh is incapable of any wrongdoing unless we choose to employ it for that which does not glorify God. In the same way that we have the power of choice to sin if we so choose, we also have the power of choice *not* to sin if we so choose! And our Redeemer took upon Himself our fallen nature that He might strengthen all who would make the latter choice. What a wonderful Savior is Jesus our Lord!

A correct understanding of the nature of sin is essential to a correct understanding of the human nature of Christ. When we understand that sin resides not in our fallen nature, but in the wrong employment of the will, then we will be able to appreciate how our Redeemer could be "in all things ... made like unto his brethren,"

---

18   Romans 6:16

19   Ellen G. White, *The Great Controversy* (Mountain View, CA: Pacific Press, 1911), 493.

20   Romans 14:23

21   Ellen G. White, *The Desire of Ages* (Mountain View, CA: Pacific Press, 1898), 125, emphasis added.

22   Ellen G. White, *The Adventist Home* (Hagerstown, MD: Review and Herald Publishing Association, 1952), 127.

[23] and be "yet without sin."[24] Then there will be no need to appeal to the misguided Augustine for unscriptural explanations of how Christ avoided the stain of so-called "original sin."

As we contemplate the important subject of the nature of Christ in the flesh, and our understanding of this matter as a people, it is good to bear in mind the counsels that have been graciously left with us. Remember, "we have nothing to fear for the future, except as we shall forget the way the Lord has led us, and His teaching in our past history."[25] What have we been taught by the Lord in our past history at this point? This is a question that has definite answers. However, before we look at those, let us consider an inspired statement that gave cautions about the dangers that were to confront the people of God in these last days.

"When men come in who would move one pin or pillar from the foundation which God has established by His Holy Spirit, let the aged men who were pioneers in our work speak plainly, and let those who are dead speak also, by the reprinting of their articles in our periodicals. Gather up the rays of divine light that God has given as He has led His people on step by step in the way of truth. This truth will stand the test of time and trial."[26]

Let us turn our attention, then, to the view of Christ's human nature long held by our church, which so many of our writers have openly confessed and boldly defended. We shall begin in 1888, when God sent a message of present truth to the church through two men chosen by Him for this purpose. Ellet Waggoner and Alonzo Jones spoke under the injunction of the Spirit of God. And their unfortunate apostasy in later years, as Ellen White forewarned,[27] provides no justification for the rejection of the truth they taught while under the influence of the Spirit of God. The message of righteousness by faith was brought to prominence among Adventists by the faithful labors of these two men, in concert with Mrs. White. But their version of righteousness by faith was quite different from the evangelical version that is popular today, and so was the Christology upon which it was constructed. Let us first consider a few statements from Waggoner.

A little thought will be sufficient to show anybody that if Christ took upon Himself the likeness of man in order that He might redeem man it must have been sinful man that He was made like, for it is sinful man that He came to redeem.... Moreover, the fact that Christ took upon Himself the flesh, not of a sinless being, but

---

23   Hebrews 2:17
24   Hebrews 4:15
25   Ellen G. White, *Life Sketches of Ellen G. White,* (Mountain View, CA: Pacific Press, 1915), 196, emphasis added.
26   Ellen G. White, *Manuscript Releases,* vol. 1 (Silver Spring, MD: Ellen G. White Estate, 1981), 55.
27   Ibid., 143.

of sinful man, that is, that the flesh which He assumed had all the weaknesses and sinful tendencies to which fallen human nature is subject, is shown by the statement that He 'was made of the seed of David *according to the flesh.*'[28]

The spotless Lamb of God, who knew no sin, was made to be sin. Sinless, yet not only counted as a sinner but actually taking upon Himself sinful nature. He was made to be sin in order that *we* might be made righteousness.[29]

Is there any one who doubts the reality of Christ's coming to live in sinful flesh, and thus showing himself master? We all believe that.... Christ has power over all flesh, and he demonstrated this when he came in the likeness of sinful, flesh, and condemned sin in the flesh.[30]

There is the testimony of Dr. Waggoner, taken entirely from the clear teaching of God's Word. As we shall now see, there was perfect theological harmony with Jones upon this point. This harmony, we understand, was indispensable in order for their joint ministry to have had the success that it did. What has Jones left behind as a witness? We are surely not short of evidence!

What kind of flesh alone is it that this world knows? *Just such flesh as you and I have.* This world does not know any other flesh of man and has not known any other since the necessity of Christ's coming was created. Therefore, as this world knows only such flesh as we have, as it is now, it is certainly true that when 'the Word was made flesh,' He was made just as flesh as ours is. It cannot be otherwise.[31]

This is a very sensible statement by Jones. This world knows no other kind of flesh than that which we all have. Therefore, for the Word to truly become flesh, He must truly become one of us, equipped with the same raw material as we all have. Jones is right in harmony with the apostle's affirmation: "For both he that sanctifieth and they who are sanctified are all of one: for which cause he is not ashamed to call them brethren."[32] Jones' testimony continues:

All the tendencies to sin that are in human flesh were in His human flesh, and not one of them was ever allowed to appear; He conquered them all. And in Him we all have victory over them all.[33]

But the wonder is that God can do that through and in *sinful* flesh. That is the mystery of God. God manifest in *sinful* flesh. In Jesus Christ as He was in sinful flesh, God has demonstrated before the universe that He can so take possession of

---

28   Ellet J. Waggoner, *Christ and His Righteousness* (Melbourne, AU: Echo Publishing Company, Ltd., 1892), 26, 27.
29   Ibid., 27, 28, emphasis added.
30   Ellet J. Waggoner, "Bible Study," *General Conference Bulletin* (April 14, 1901), 200, 223.
31   A. T. Jones, "The Third Angel's Message-1," *General Conference Bulletin* (1895), 232, emphasis added.
32   Hebrews 2:11
33   A. T. Jones, "The Third Angel's Message-1," *General Conference Bulletin* (1895), 267..

sinful flesh as to manifest His own presence, His power, and His glory, instead of sin manifesting itself.[34]

Surely we can understand why Satan would never tolerate such a doctrine. This is a matter that exposes him before the entire intelligent universe. Such a comprehensive failure is he that not even on his own turf (sinful flesh) could he defeat the Lord! He had thirty-three years to attempt it, and he lost catastrophically. And what is his new strategy? Ah, easy! Convince the world that Jesus cheated in the great controversy! Accuse God of conspiring with Jesus to deceive the entire universe by making us think that God became man, when, in reality, He only became a kind of angel-man or a sort of quasi-human and not the real article. Tell the world that Christ overcame because His nature was not really fallen. In other words, the Bible is an untruth, for Christ was made only *in some things* like unto His brethren, not "in all things," as Paul affirms. O father of lies, how far will you go? Yet the lie itself bothers me much less than the willingness of good people to believe it!

We will now turn our attention to the teaching of W. W. Prescott, a former vice president of the General Conference and respected educator in Adventist history. Concerning the nature of Christ in the flesh, he wrote:

Jesus Christ had exactly the same flesh that we bear, flesh of sin, flesh in which *we* sin, however, in which He did not sin, but He bore *our* sins in that flesh.[35]

Jesus Christ came for that work [salvation]; and in order to do it, He came, not where man was before he fell, but where man was after He fell…. When Christ comes to help man out of the pit, He does not come to the edge of the pit and look over, and say, Come up here, and I will help you back…. Jesus Christ come[s] right down where he is, and meets him there. He takes his flesh and becomes a brother to him.[36]

Waggoner, Jones, and Prescott are just a meager sampling of the many Adventist leaders, pastors, editors, administrators, and other workers prior to the 1950s who believed and taught that Christ took the nature of fallen humanity when He came in the flesh.[37] But now, let us consider yet another writer who generously contributed more than 400 statements affirming that Christ took the nature of fallen man. The writer of which I speak is none other than Ellen Gould White, pioneer and prophetess of God to the remnant church. What did *she* have to say about the human nature of Christ? What did she understand by "the Word was made flesh?"

---

34 Ibid., 303.
35 W. W. Prescott, "The Word Became Flesh," *The Bible Echo Articles,* 1896.
36 Ibid.
37 Others include luminaries such as James White, Uriah Smith, S. N. Haskell, J. H. Durland, A. V. Farnsworth, J. E. Evans, M. C. Wilcox, W. N. Glenn, G. W. Reaser, R. A. Underwood, J. L. Schuler, G. B. Thompson, W. Howard James, L. A. Reed, Meade MacGuire, William Wirth, W. H. Branson, C. P. Bollman, Miriam M. Hay, and countless others. The book *The Word Was Made Flesh* by Ralph Larson gives more than one thousand quotations that prove the unity of the denomination on this point from 1852 to 1952.

Here are just a few of her clearest statements on the topic:

It would have been an almost infinite humiliation for the Son of God to take man's nature, even when Adam stood in his innocence in Eden. But Jesus accepted humanity when the race had been weakened by four thousand years of sin. Like every child of Adam He accepted the results of the working of the great law of heredity. What these results were is shown in the history of His earthly ancestors. He came with such a heredity *to share our sorrows and temptations, and to give us the example of a sinless life.*[38]

It was not a make-believe humanity that Christ took upon Himself. He took human nature and lived human nature.... He was compassed with infirmities ... just that which you may be He was in human nature. He took our infirmities. He was not only made flesh, but He was made in the likeness of sinful flesh.[39]

In taking upon Himself man's nature in its fallen condition, Christ did not in the least participate in its sin.[40]

Now let us consider carefully the preceding statement. Is it not obvious that such a statement would make absolutely no sense if the human nature assumed by the Savior was indeed the sinless nature of Adam before the fall? Take careful note also of the quotations that follow, for they express that it was by divine design that Christ took the nature of fallen human beings, and that this was the only way for the plan of salvation to be effectual.

It was in the order of God that Christ should take upon Himself the form and nature of fallen man, that He might be made perfect through suffering, and himself endure the strength of Satan's fierce temptations, that He might understand how to succor those who should be tempted.[41]

The great work of redemption could be carried out by the Redeemer only as He took the place of fallen man.... When Adam was assailed by the tempter, none of the effects of sin were upon him, but he was surrounded by the glories of Eden. But it was not thus with Jesus; for, bearing the infirmities of degenerate humanity, He entered the wilderness to cope with the mighty foe.[42]

We have provided here five out of 400 statements from the inspired servant of the Lord on our subject, in addition to others found elsewhere in this discourse. We feel no further proof is required to establish what she believed and taught. Let us

---

38   Ellen G. White, *The Desire of Ages* (Mountain View, CA: Pacific Press, 1898), 49, emphasis added.
39   Ellen G. White, *Letter 106,* (1896).
40   Ellen G. White, *Selected Messages,* book 1 (Washington, D.C.: Review and Herald Publishing Association, 1958), 256.
41   Ellen G. White, *Spirit of Prophecy,* vol. 2 (Battle Creek, MI: Seventh-day Adventist Publishing Association, 1877), 39.
42   Ellen G. White, "The Temptation in the Wilderness," *The Bible Echo* (1892), 338.

then complete our evidence with two quotes from the *Sabbath School Quarterly* and a well-known book of ours, *Bible Readings for the Home Circle*.

In 1921, this subject was discussed in the *Sabbath School Quarterly*. The first quarter edition carried the following affirmation: "Christ assumed, not the original unfallen, but our fallen humanity. In this second experiment, He stood not precisely where Adam before Him had, but, as has already been said, with immense odds against Him...."[43]

Consider this final statement, found in the third edition of that which has been our standard doctrinal book, *Bible Readings for the Home Circle*:

In His humanity Christ partook of our sinful nature. If not then He was not made like unto his brethren, was not in all points tempted like as we are, did not overcome as we have to overcome, and is not therefore the complete and perfect Saviour man needs, and must have to be saved. The idea that Christ was born of an immaculate, sinless mother, inherited no tendencies to sin, removes Him from the realm of a fallen world, and from the very place where help is needed. On his human side, Christ inherited just what every child of Adam inherited, a sinful nature. On the Divine side, from His very conception He was begotten and born of the Spirit. And all this was done to place mankind on vantage ground, and to demonstrate that in the same way everyone who is born of the Spirit, may gain like victories over sin in His own sinful flesh.... Without this birth, there can be no victory over temptation, and no salvation from sin.[44]

Having considered all this, I wish to now raise a rather pertinent and provocative question: what does the human nature of Christ have to do with the third angel's message of Revelation 14 that urgently calls us to go to every nation, warning them against the worship of the beast and his image and the reception of his mark? Perhaps, as we contemplate as grave a matter as this, it would be well to go again to that message, and see what it says. This we shall do without delay.

> *To worship this beast is to choose to follow its dogmas in place of the teachings of the authoritative Word of God.*

And the third angel followed them, saying with a loud voice, If any man worship the beast and his image, and receive his mark in his forehead, or in his hand, the same shall drink of the wine of the wrath of God, which is poured out without

---

43   *Sabbath School Lesson Quarterly,* Senior Division, First Quarter (Mountain View, CA: Pacific Press, 1921), 16.

44   *Bible Readings for the Home Circle,* 3rd ed. (Review and Herald Publishing Association, 1936), 115, 116.

mixture into the cup of his indignation; and he shall be tormented with fire and brimstone in the presence of the holy angels, and in the presence of the Lamb: and the smoke of their torment ascendeth up for ever and ever: and they have no rest day nor night, who worship the beast and his image, and whosoever receiveth the mark of his name. Here is the patience of the saints: here are they that keep the commandments of God, and the faith of Jesus.[45]

Seeing that we have before us the most solemn and startling warning ever issued by God to mortals, it behooves each soul to know what or who is this beast, what constitutes his worship, and how it may be avoided, for it is said that those who worship the beast and his image, and thereby receive his mark, shall be visited with the wrath of the living God. We have been duly cautioned by the apostle Paul that "it is a fearful thing to fall into the hands of the living God."[46]

We concur with the great cloud of witnesses of eminent Protestant scholars whose careful analysis of the biblical evidence have led them to the conclusion that the beast here mentioned by the apostle is none other than the Roman papacy. And to worship this beast is to choose to follow its dogmas in place of the teachings of the authoritative Word of God.

The apostle John, whose announcement of Christ's incarnation provided our launching-pad for this study, not only conveys the warning against the beast in Revelation 13 but before this, in his epistle, he also had something to say about that power. Correctly applying the term "antichrist" to this very system (and indeed to every other system employed by Satan to oppose the true work of the gospel), John warned that it would seek to corrupt the biblical doctrine of the incarnation of the Savior. Let us consider again his words:

Beloved, believe not every spirit, but try the spirits whether they are of God: because many false prophets are gone out into the world. Hereby know ye the Spirit of God: Every spirit that confesseth that Jesus Christ is come in the flesh is of God: And every spirit that confesseth not that Jesus Christ is come in the flesh is not of God: and this is that spirit of antichrist, whereof ye have heard that it should come; and even now already is it in the world.[47]

That antichrist power, or the beast which John later saw in vision, would teach that Jesus Christ did not come in the flesh. This does not mean, as some suppose, that the antichrist would teach that Christ did not have a real physical body. If that were the case, then there would be no antichrist, for the Papacy (which we know to be the antichrist that "should come") like all Christian confessions, teaches that Christ was a real

---

45   Revelation 14:9–12
46   Hebrews 10:31
47   1 John 4:1–3

historical person. If the coming "in the flesh" of which John speaks is merely the appearance of Christ in a human body, we would be forced to accept that the papal power "is of God." But such a conclusion contradicts the clear testimony of the Word of God. To unlock the puzzle of John's warning, we must take into account the secondary meaning of the word "flesh" as used by John and many other Bible writers. The word employed in the Greek is *sarx*, which denotes not just the physical flesh and bones but also the human nature of fallen humankind. John's identifying mark for the antichrist power is that it would hold a doctrine that denies that Christ took fallen flesh (*sarx*) in His incarnation (Latin: *in carnis*). Could this be true? Does Roman Catholicism really teach that Christ took upon himself "holy flesh" and not sinful flesh as the Bible affirms? It is most definitely true, as we shall now see from its own statements:

Through the centuries the Church has become ever more aware that Mary, 'full of grace' through God, was redeemed from the moment of her conception. That is what the dogma of the Immaculate Conception confesses, as Pope Pius IX proclaimed in 1854: 'The most Blessed Virgin Mary was, from the first moment of her conception, by a singular grace and privilege of almighty God and by virtue of the merits of Jesus Christ, Savior of the human race, preserved immune from all stain of original sin.'[48]

The same doctrine is repeated in the following statement by a Catholic priest: "In teaching that Mary was conceived immaculate, the Catholic Church teaches that from the very moment of her conception, the Blessed Virgin Mary was free from all stain of original sin. This simply means that from the beginning, she was in a state of grace, sharing in God's own life, and that she was free from the sinful inclinations which have beset human nature after the fall."[49] This other statement from the Catechism is quite enlightening: "What the Catholic faith believes about Mary is based on what it believes *about Christ*, and what it teaches about Mary illumines in turn its faith in Christ."[50]

The counsel given by the apostle John was not lost upon the Seventh-day Adventist Church. At the General Conference Session in 1901, Ellet Waggoner, addressing the assembled delegates, stated the following: "Did you ever hear of the Roman Catholic doctrine of the immaculate conception? ... The doctrine of the immaculate conception is that Mary, the mother of Jesus, was born sinless. Why? — Ostensibly to magnify Jesus; really the work of the devil to put a wide gulf between Jesus the Saviour of men, and the men whom he came to save, so that one could not

---

48   *Catechism of the Catholic Church*, part 1, section 2, chapter 2, article 3.
49   William G. Most, "Mary's Immaculate Conception," EWTN Global Catholic Network, http://bit.ly/1d1jI4B (accessed December 17, 2013).
50   *Catechism of the Catholic Church,* part 1, section 2, chapter 2, article 3, emphasis added.

pass over to the other. That is all. We need to settle, every one of us, whether we are out of the church of Rome or not."[51]

We thank God for the faithful witness of the *Sabbath School Quarterly*, which again echoed the voice of dear old John in warning against papal falsehoods such as the one under consideration. We read with interest from another old edition:

What is the teaching of modern Babylon concerning this same fundamental doctrine? By the dogma of the immaculate conception of the virgin Mary, Rome teaches that the mother of Jesus was preserved from the stain of original sin, and that she had sinless flesh. Consequently she was separated from the rest of humanity. As a result of this separation of Jesus from sinful flesh, the Roman priesthood has been instituted in order that there may be some one to mediate between Christ and the sinner.[52]

Thus by shutting Christ away from the same flesh and blood which we have ... modern Babylon really denies the vital truth of Christianity, *although pretending to teach it.* Such is 'the mystery of iniquity.'[53]

The *Sabbath School Quarterly* editors of the early 1900s seemed to have understood quite well the following caution given by the Lord's messenger: "We make many mistakes because of the erroneous views of the human nature of our Lord. When we give to His human nature a power that it is not possible for man to have in his conflicts with Satan, we destroy the completeness of His humanity."[54] To do such a work is to be in league with the very man of sin and to plant our feet ever so firmly on the perilous path to perdition.

Would we heed the warning of the third angel's message? Would we avoid the reception of the mark of the beast? It will not suffice to reject one papal

> *In a time when the whole world wonders after the beast by the reception of its spurious doctrines, we must stand on the Bible and the Bible alone.*

heresy (Sunday sacredness) and embrace another (immaculate flesh of Christ). A complete break with falsehood is what is required. John has admonished us. The very fact that this teaching is of Catholic origin ought to serve as ample warning to every thinking person, for this system exalts the traditions of humanity above the Word of God. Will God's people also wonder after the beast? Is this one of Satan's traps to

---

51   Ellet J. Waggoner, sermon, General Conference Session, Battle Creek, MI, April 16, 1901..
52   *Sabbath School Lesson Quarterly*, Senior Division, Second Quarter (Mountain View, CA: Pacific Press, 1913), 25.
53   Ibid., 26. (emphasis added)
54   Ellen G. White, *The Seventh-day Adventist Bible Commentary*, vol. 7 (Washington DC: Review and Herald Publish Association, 1957), 929.

deceive many of the very elect? These are no trifling matters! Will good men and women indeed pledge allegiance to a false Christ—the Christ of Papal Rome?

In a time when the whole world wonders after the beast by the reception of its spurious doctrines, we must stand on the Bible and the Bible alone. What E. J. Waggoner said in 1901 is even more relevant today. We must decide, every one of us, whether or not we are truly out of the church of Rome. Truth has not been hidden from our eyes. It is not hard to know the way of the Lord. The time is even now upon us when humankind will know who are those that serve the Lord and who are those that do not.

When John tells us that the Word became flesh, he does not merely mean that Jesus took on a human appearance. He would not have us understand that Christ pretended to become a man. He means that Christ became a full human being. He did not come shielded in some kind of moral and spiritual protector suit. His only protection from defilement was His relationship with the Father—a protection that has, through Him, been made available to every fallen human being. His mission was not to prove what a man with special privileges could do, but what the weakest of mortals, encumbered by the liabilities of the flesh (*sarx*) could achieve by the power of divine grace. What John frankly affirms, Paul clarifies more eloquently by telling us that the Savior took upon Himself the likeness of sinful flesh. Thus says the Word, and thus we believe with all gratitude and praise to our all-wise Creator.

In a previously cited statement by the Lord's servant, we were told what to do when the world would come in trying to subtly move away the pillars and the foundations upon which this movement has been built. We were told to dig up the archives and publish again the truth that was given to us under the mighty moving of the Spirit of God. This we have done, and we are unmoved in our conviction that the true Word shall win in the end. As has been said, "This truth will stand the test of time and trial."[55]

Again I say, what a wonderful Savior is Jesus! He knows my sorrows, and He knows my woes. He understands the bitter battles and straining struggles in which I am daily engaged. He is not a stranger to the devil's devious devices. When upon tired knees and with painful pathos and trembling tones, I say to Him, "My soul is sorely tempted, and my heart trembles at the mighty power of the enemy." No one needs to explain to Him precisely what I mean. I have no need of any human intermediary. He has walked this way before. He has lived in sinful flesh—triumphantly lived in sinful flesh. By the power of God He conquered, and in that power, so may I. There is hope for humanity in that Word that was made "in the likeness of sinful flesh." Glory to the Incarnate Son, who took my human nature, and in that nature overcame, so that I might be a partaker of *His* divine nature by the good grace of the Almighty!

---

55   Ellen G. White, *Manuscript Releases*, vol. 1 (Silver Spring, MD: Ellen G. White Estate, 1981), 55.

Providenciales, Turks and Caicos Islands

"Joy in the night is great, but joy in the morning is even greater still!"

Prologue

I have always been a believer in the practical things in life, and this is a principle that I carried with me throughout my years in the theological seminary. Never content with merely what could be learned from books and classroom lectures, I was always on the lookout for opportunities to put into action the knowledge I was acquiring. This was particularly true when it came to preaching, for I felt that this was an area where I was constantly in special need of proper and practical preparation. This was due to the fact that, up to the end of my sophomore year, I was still unsure of whether or not I had what it took to achieve any semblance of success as a preacher.

I remember sitting beside a friend at the Halse Hall Seventh-day Adventist Church in Clarendon one Sabbath and listening to a moving sermon by the preacher. I was about eighteen years old at the time and had recently been interviewed by Richard 'Richie B' Burgess on Radio Jamaica concerning my participation in the National Schools Debating Competition and my aspirations for the future. In that interview I spoke of my dream of becoming an engineer of some sort—one of the many dreams that came and went during those vacillating teenage years. But as I listened to that preacher and felt the power of his words, I was at once overwhelmed by two contrasting emotions—an intense desire to minister the Word, and an acute despair at my utter incompetence to do so! In tones that betrayed my desperation, I said to my friend, "I just wish that I knew how to preach!"

Sometimes God does most through those who think themselves the least qualified. Humility is a jewel that is highly esteemed in heaven, though often scorned and despised among mortals. This is a lesson that I have come to learn in a variety of ways, and it has led me to trust God for better results in the future after completing my first week of prayer series in Westmoreland in December 1999.

That trust eventually paid off, and by May 2003, I was prepared to take on the first overseas evangelistic tour, a few months before my graduation. The previous year I had gone to Mexico to preach, but that was only one sermon in a two-week campaign with a different speaker every night. On this particular occasion, I was responsible for two three-week programs to be held in the Turks and Caicos Islands, where Pastor Peter Kerr, president at the time, had graciously invited me.

As we began to make plans for the activities of the summer, Pastor Kerr asked whether I had a colleague who might be interested in accompanying me to the islands to help with the summer's work. I did have such a colleague. My roommate and close friend Dorian Kelly was happy to accept the invitation. The feeling was mutual between us that this mission trip would provide invaluable experience in a tough field, even as we approached the end of our preparation for ministry and our anticipated introduction into full-time service. And it was thus proved.

We were warmly welcomed by Pastors Kerr and Leonardo Rahming, who served at the time as an associate pastor in a number of the churches on the islands. After a brief respite, we were dispatched to our first assignment on the island of North Caicos. We found a small but enthusiastic group of brethren there under the leadership of Sister Gardiner, who helped us coordinate our efforts and graciously hosted us in her home during the three-week stay.

As Kelly and I made our visitation rounds during the daytime and alternated with the preaching responsibilities in the nights, we were kindly cautioned by Pastor Rahming against any expectation of baptizing scores of people as is often the case in our home country, Jamaica. He tried to sensitize us to the different order of evangelistic work in the Turks and Caicos Islands—an undertaking that he aptly referred to as "chipping at the rock." We quickly grasped the concept, and we rejoiced with the brethren when three young children were baptized at the end of the campaign!

With the first leg of the tour completed, it was now time to focus on the larger island of Providenciales and the Blue Hills Church. Here, another challenging but fulfilling experience awaited us. Kelly and I decided to give the same sermons as in the North Caicos series and to persist with the preaching rotation plan we had followed in the previous campaign. This was a major blessing, as it saved us from burnout due to the hours spent in the field during the days. These campaigns helped us to appreciate more the immense blessings that can come when evangelists make the extra effort to visit in the communities they minister to—a practice that has continued with us to the present time.

The Blue Hills event will be especially remembered for a number of reasons. I would like to mention what I think to be the most outstanding. During our stay in North Caicos, a Trinidadian music teacher who worked at the local high school visited the campaign. Her religious background was non-Protestant, but she was deeply impressed by a lecture that Kelly gave on the Sabbath question. She did not make a decision to be baptized then, but on the final day of the campaign in Providenciales when the call was made for those who desire baptism to come forward, this dear lady showed up, having flown over from North Caicos, and indicated that she had decided to surrender her life to the Lord!

The sermon that I share in this chapter is an updated rendering of the one I gave to bring the curtains down on this eventful trip to the Turks and Caicos Islands. It comes from the same text as *Joy in the Night*, but this time, the focus is not the night, but the long-awaited morning. Joy in the morning is the principal promise of the Bible. It was a fitting word to conclude our mission trip then, and it is an even more fitting word with which to conclude this book.

The Message: Joy in the Morning

"Weeping may endure for a night, but joy cometh in the morning." Psalm 30:5

The word "joy," in the thinking of this preacher, is synonymous with the word "gospel," for the gospel is that which we have come to know as the good news, and the good news is ever a source of joy to those who are blessed to receive it. I have discovered, in my investigation and daily meditation, that joy is a recurring theme that runs throughout the Sacred Scriptures. At the very beginning when God brought this world into existence, it was a most joyous occasion, for we are told that "the morning stars sang together, and all the sons of God shouted for joy."[1] When humankind deviated from the path of purity, and it became necessary to put in motion that divine intervention known as the plan of salvation, at the appointed hour, an angel was sent with an announcement to the humble sheep minders, and he said, "Fear not: for, behold, I bring you good tidings of great joy … For unto you is born this day in the city of David a Saviour, which is Christ the Lord."[2] And when we come to the Revelation, the restoration of all things to their first estate, we find the triumphant people of God surrounded by the most blissful circumstances. Of them it is said: "God shall wipe away all tears from their eyes; and there shall be no more death, neither sorrow, nor

---

1   Job 38:7
2   Luke 2:10, 11

crying, neither shall there be any more pain: for the former things are passed away."[3]

As I think upon this glorious vision of the prophet John, and the promised wiping of all tears from the eyes of those who have patiently endured the night of their pilgrimage on earth, I cannot but reflect again upon the words of the inspired poet. We recall with interest that he said: "Weeping may endure for a night, but joy cometh in the morning." Indeed, we began this journey with David. We checked in with him along the way. And as we approach our port of landing, I feel it is to our benefit to consult with him again. Before we go, we would understand both the measure and the meaning of this "joy in the morning."

I grew up in a modest village called Lampard near the town of Frankfield in Jamaica. Every Sabbath morning I would walk down the hill in the company of my father, mother, and siblings to attend the worship service at the Frankfield Seventh-day Adventist Church, where we were members. It was not a large church, but it taught us the faith of Jesus. It was not a perfect church, but it showed us the way to a perfect God. It was not known for its splendor or for its stunning sophistication, but it planted the seed of truth in our hearts. It was not a church overflowing with financial resources, but it understood the value of fellowship—and not just spiritual fellowship but social fellowship as well. So when the holiday seasons came around, we knew that it was time for social fellowship, and the annual beach excursion was a fixture on our agenda.

> *While the night lasts, it is good to have joy to sustain us and maintain us. But no night lasts forever. By and by, the golden morning will come.*

As a boy of about nine or ten years, I was privileged to go for the first time. Almost invariably Mr. Simpson's Metro Bus Company was the preferred mode of transportation. This was a source of delight for us young boys, especially if we were able to secure the service of a special unit that he had, known as "Ultimate Power," or "The 16"—a specially modified autobus that boasted a (what we believed to be) sixteen-speed trailer engine and a very colorful outside paint job.

On this occasion, our destination was Negril, Westmoreland—a popular tourist town on the island's north coast. It would take us at least three hours to make the trip, or less, depending on which of Mr. Simpson's flamboyant sons was the driver. I could not wait for my turn to climb up the steps and find a window seat, and once found, it was then time to become obsessed with another pressing matter—Negril.

---

3   Revelation 21:4

How far away was our destination, and when exactly were we going to get there?

Up through the twists and turns of John's Hall we went. We passed through the pleasant James Hill, went along by the breezy plains of Cave Valley, and down through Brown's Town and on to Discovery Bay. Are we there yet? When do we get to Negril?

A semblance of that boyish anxiety resurfaces when I read that "weeping may endure for a night, but joy cometh in the morning." For three long hours, my desire was to be in Negril, but my reality was a less-than-comfortable seat in a belching bus that never seemed to be going fast enough (for me, that is). And on the spiritual side, our desire is for the morning, but our reality is the night of weeping where the hours seem to creep by and the earnest longing for daybreak intensifies with every moment that passes.

As for the night, we have been told how to deal with it. It is not our principal subject for the present treatise. The recipe for *Joy in the Night* has already been broadcasted for the benefit of all. But we shall not be on the bus much longer. Even now the coastline begins to take form on the horizon. While the night lasts, it is good to have joy to sustain us and maintain us. But no night lasts forever. By and by, the golden morning will come.

But what is this "morning," which we all await with fond expectations and earnest anticipation? What is the "day" that Paul tells us "is at hand"? It is none other than that most glorious event that has been the hope of the church ever since these wonderful words were spoken by the Savior: "Let not your heart be troubled: ye believe in God, believe also in me.... If I go and prepare a place for you, I will come again, and receive you unto myself; that where I am, there ye may be also."[4] It is the day of the Lord, soon to break upon us, when "this same Jesus, which is taken up from you into heaven, shall so come in like manner as ye have seen him go into heaven,"[5] and "the Lord himself shall descend from heaven with a shout, with the voice of the archangel, and with the trump of God."[6]

The return of Jesus Christ to this earth in power and great glory can easily be classified as the doctrine of all doctrines in the Word of God. As the inspired writer observes, "about His coming cluster the glories of that 'restitution of all things, which God hath spoken by the mouth of all His holy prophets since the world began.'"[7]

My purpose in this presentation is simply to highlight three captivating characteristics of the morning, make a brief comparison between the joy of the night and that of the morning, and then leave with you a few parting words of cheering

---

4   John 14:1, 3
5   Acts 1:11
6   1 Thessalonians 4:16
7   Ellen G. White, *The Great Controversy* (Mountain View, CA: Pacific Press, 1911), 301.

Christian hope.

The first feature of the morning that has impressed me deeply and to which I now call your most careful attention, is the fact that we are ignorant of its *timing*. We know that it is coming, but we know not precisely when it will appear. This calls for the most solemn contemplation of every child of God, for it is an irreversible fact that the joy of the morning is only for those who undertake the necessary preparation. For sure "joy cometh in the morning," but this is a conditional promise that will be only fulfilled to those who are found ready.

Here we find a remarkable distinction between the natural and the spiritual. When we go to sleep at night, we do so knowing that the night will pass and the morning will surely follow. This routine has continued uninterrupted ever since "the evening and the morning were the first day."[8] Not only that, but we also have developed the ability to predict with fair accuracy the timing of the morning's arrival. We can say, "The sun will rise tomorrow at 6:30 a.m., and it will set at 6:25 p.m." It is a natural fact that morning follows night, and when the sun spreads its golden rays over the earth, both the just and the unjust receive the benefits of its warmth and light. But in that great getting-up morning that we so eagerly await, when the Sun of Righteousness shall arise, a different principle will be put into operation. The wicked will not be able to withstand the glory of the divine presence. Those who have never allowed Jesus to be their only joy and song will have no part with the redeemed throng when the morning comes. Then it will be seen that Brother David was right: "The ungodly shall not stand in the judgment, nor sinners in the congregation of the righteous."[9]

It may bother some folk to hear such somber words as these in a sermon that is centered on joy. Be not dismayed, dear friend of mine, for it is in keeping with the spirit of this sermon that I would warn you against the stealthy strategies of the enemy. He is in the business of blocking you from that joy that was purchased for you at Calvary. If he can only get a small advantage, he would summon all his demons to build up a wall between you and your God. How can he build up such a wall that would prevent you from entering into that eternal rest prepared by God for you from the foundation of the world? There is but one answer, dear child of God, and the prophet Isaiah expresses it with great eloquence: "But your iniquities have separated between you and your God, and your sins have hid his face from you, that he will not hear."[10]

Do not be alarmed that God should speak so sternly when our subject is joy in

8   Genesis 1:5
9   Psalm 1:5
10   Isaiah 59:2

the morning, for in His infinite wisdom He has chosen this as His method to keep the eyes of His dear children fixed on the eternal prize.

No one will argue against the assertion that the twenty-first chapter of Revelation is one of the most pleasant passages in the entire Bible. It gives to us an enthralling preview of the morning and the joy that is stored up for the finally faithful. It speaks of the new heaven and the new earth. John sees the New Jerusalem descend from heaven in all her celestial glory. As much as human words allow, he paints for us a most wonderful picture of the joy that is reserved for the redeemed. But there is space in that beautiful chapter for a few gracious words of caution, and though they provoke us to solemn thought, we believe that they belong there, and there is not a sensible person upon the face of the whole earth who would argue for their exclusion.

John tells us: "But the fearful, and unbelieving, and the abominable, and murderers, and whoremongers, and sorcerers, and idolaters, and all liars, shall have their part in the lake which burneth with fire and brimstone."[11] "And there shall in no wise enter into it any thing that defileth, neither whatsoever worketh abomination, or maketh a lie: but they which are written in the Lamb's book of life."[12]

In these words John only repeats the sentiments of his Master, with whom he walked for three and a half years. He heard Jesus say, "Take heed to yourselves, lest at any time your hearts be overcharged with surfeiting, and drunkenness, and cares of this life, and so that day come upon you unawares."[13] He heard Jesus say, "Watch therefore, for ye know neither the day nor the hour wherein the Son of man cometh."[14]

Here again are the words of the inspired writer: "We believe without a doubt that Christ is soon coming.... When He comes He is not to cleanse us of our sins, to remove from us the defects in our characters, or to cure us from the infirmities of our tempers and dispositions. If wrought for us at all, this work will all be accomplished before that time. When the Lord comes, those who are holy will be holy still. Those who have preserved their bodies and spirits in holiness, in sanctification and honor, will then receive the finishing touch of immortality. But those who are unjust, unsanctified, and filthy will remain so forever. No work will then be done for them to remove their defects and give them holy characters. The Refiner does not then sit to pursue His refining process and remove their sins and their corruption. This is all to be done in these hours of probation. It is *now* that this work is to be accomplished for us."[15]

---

11   Revelation 21:8
12   Revelation 21:27
13   Luke 21:34
14   Matthew 25:13
15   Ellen G. White, *Testimonies for the Church*, vol. 2 (Mountain View, CA: Pacific Press, 1871), 355.

I must warn my hearers against that fallacy of a doctrine that assures humanity of salvation in their sins. There is no such thing, dear friend of mine. Let not Satan lure you to continue in your sins until Jesus comes. The preaching of such a doctrine from the sacred pulpit is evidence that we are even now in earth's darkest hour.

The precise hour of the morning's arrival is not the principal concern of God's people. There is no need to set times or invent fanciful chronological schemes. Preparation is the key issue of concern to us. We may not know the hour when the day will dawn, but this ignorance will be no disadvantage to those who are waiting and watching.

A second feature of the morning that I feel I must highlight is the fact of its *imminence*. We have alluded to this fact before, but here I want to explore a bit more the nearness of the morning for which we are praying. Long has been the night that we have endured. But as we are told by the Lord's apostle, "Now it is high time to awake out of sleep: for now is our salvation nearer than when we believed. The night is far spent, the day is at hand."[16] "The great day of the LORD is near, it is near, and hasteth greatly, even the voice of the day of the LORD."[17]

Again, in that amazing book of hope—Revelation—there is a threefold blessing offered in the very first chapter, and the reason for this blessing is given at the very end of the text. It says: "Blessed is he that readeth, and they that hear the words of this prophecy, and keep those things which are written therein: for the time is at hand."[18] And in the last chapter of the same love letter, the Lord Himself says to us, "Behold, I come quickly; and my reward is with me, to give every man according as his work shall be."[19]

To know just how near we are to that most glorious morning we need only to look at the signs that indicate its proximity. As Jesus spoke of the conditions existing in the world just prior to His return, He said, "Likewise also as it was in the days of Lot ... Even thus shall it be in the day when the Son of man is revealed."[20] How was it in the days of Lot? Here is an answer: "They did eat, they drank, they bought, they sold, they planted, they builded; But the same day that Lot went out of Sodom it rained fire and brimstone from heaven, and destroyed them all."[21]

But this is not all that the Bible tells us about the days of Lot. In Genesis 19 we read the following about the grossly immoral condition of the world in Lot's day: "And there came two angels to Sodom at even; and Lot sat in the gate of Sodom: and

16   Romans 13:11, 12
17   Zephaniah 1:14
18   Revelation 1:3
19   Revelation 22:12
20   Luke 17:28, 30
21   Luke 17:28, 29

Lot seeing them rose up to meet them ... And he said, behold now, my lords, turn in, I pray you, into your servant's house, and tarry all night, and wash your feet, and ye shall rise up early, and go on your ways.... And he pressed upon them greatly; and they turned in unto him, and entered into his house ... But before they lay down, the men of the city, even the men of Sodom, compassed the house round, both old and young, all the people from every quarter. And they called unto Lot, and said unto him, Where are the men which came in to thee this night? bring them out unto us, that we may know them."[22]

One of the sure signs of the imminence of the coming of Christ is the astounding favor with which sexual perversity, and especially sodomy, is viewed in the world to-day. We have presidents who pride themselves in their success in placing such persons in public office. More and more countries are passing legislation that permits homosexuals to marry, and in some cases, even to adopt children! Merely upholding the biblical truth, which condemns this illicit lifestyle, is enough to bring upon God's people the charge of participating in "hate speech." So-called ministers of the gospel—the reputed spiritual guardians of the peo-

> *To understand the results of a departure from Bible truth, one need look no further than to the divisive factions of modern Christendom, all of which claim to have the oracles of God.*

ple—are themselves immersed in the mire. The plague is more rampant than it has ever been. That which warranted the utter destruction of Sodom and Gomorrah is now defended today under the pretense of upholding human rights. I feel that the Lord cannot bear to see the corruption much longer, and ere long He will arise to cleanse the earth of all its revolting perversion.

Another remarkable sign of the nearness of the morning is the startling accuracy with which Paul's words concerning the corruption of the truth are being fulfilled. Said the apostle: "Now the Spirit speaketh expressly, that in the latter times some shall depart from the faith, giving heed to seducing spirits, and doctrines of devils."[23] "For the time will come when they will not endure sound doctrine; but after their own lusts shall they heap to themselves teachers, having itching ears; and they shall turn away their ears from the truth, and shall be turned unto fables."[24]

Indeed, religious fables are the order of the day. Unmixed, cutting truth is no

---

22 Genesis 19:1-5
23 1 Timothy 4:1
24 2 Timothy 4:3, 4

longer desired. Men have no interest in hearing that they need a reformation of life. They desire an accommodating Christ, one that accepts them without demanding too many adjustments. To understand the results of a departure from Bible truth, one need look no further than to the divisive factions of modern Christendom, all of which claim to have the oracles of God. Every wind of doctrine blows. Truth and falsehood sit crowned together upon the pedestal of humanity's hearts. The most popular preachers are those who least rely upon the Bible. Paul saw it all. The morning is near in verity.

And what can be said about religious intolerance? Already we can see it slowly raising its ugly head. Our age is lauded as the age of enlightenment and freedom of religion, but can we not see the stealthy emergence of a determined and powerful antagonism to true religious freedom? Speaking of the formation of a tyrannical, persecuting, global, political, and religious power that would arise in the end-time scenario, the apostle John said, "And he had power to give life unto the image of the beast, that the image of the beast should both speak, and cause that as many as would not worship the image of the beast should be killed."[25] Jesus has warned us that such a time would come. The Lord declared, "Yea, the time cometh, that whosoever killeth you will think that he doeth God service."[26]

There are those who are tempted to believe that such terrible scenes are not possible in an enlightened age such as ours. But we think the evidence tells an opposite story. The plot is even now in place for an exact fulfillment of what the Bible predicts. Only a suitable pretext remains, and I believe it will be found not long hence.

Whether we believe it or not, the mystery of iniquity has long been working, even though millions have no clue of its progress! Sign after sign heralds the approach of the morning. It is time for us to look up; the redemption of the children of God draws nigh!

> *Joy in the night is the joy that we can have in this world, but joy in the morning is the joy that will be ours in the world to come.*

Now let us briefly dwell upon my third observation concerning the morning. There seems to exist an element of *uniqueness* about this particular morning. I have noticed that when the morning comes, it will be the dawning of a day that is unlike any other, for the day-night cycle as we know it will be forever ended. The

25   Revelation 13:15
26   John 16:2

Scriptures tells us that there will be "no night there."[27]

I find it to be a most fascinating thought that from that day onwards there will be no night there. Literally and symbolically, there will be no night there. Whether we speak naturally or spiritually, there will be no night there. Whether nights of physical distress or nights of emotional perplexity, the Word of God affirms that there will be no night there. Whether nights of bitter disappointment or nights of cruel abandonment, Inspiration assures us that there will be no night there. Whether nights of insupportable loneliness or nights of unspeakable sorrow, the Holy Bible testifies that there will be no night there. Whether nights of withering sickness or nights of horrifying death, the Sacred Scroll promises that there will be no night there!

No night there to vex us and perplex us! No night there to depress us and oppress us! No night there to encage us and enrage us! No night there to enshroud us and becloud us!

This causes me to contemplate carefully a most important spiritual principle that has to do with the function of joy in the night. I see joy in the night, not as an end in itself, but rather as a means to an end. In other words, do not get too comfortable with the joy that you have in the night. There is a fuller joy that God desires to give. You see, joy in the night is the joy that we can have in this world, but joy in the morning is the joy that will be ours in the world to come.

Right now I may have some joy on the inside, for the peace of Jesus abides there. But I have no real joy on the outside, for I still live in a world of wickedness and woe. However, as David says, "In thy presence is fulness of joy; at thy right hand there are pleasures for evermore."[28] This tells me that I can experience joy whenever I come into the presence of God. When His Spirit is in me and His angels surround me and His love encircles me, there is a joy that I feel inside. But it cannot be "fullness of joy," until the morning comes and I enter into His very presence and sit at His right hand.

The joy that we have down here is an incomplete joy. The joy that we have down here is an introductory joy. The joy that we have down here is a precursory joy. The joy that we have down here is a provisional joy. We must never forget that the morning is coming. Joy in the night is great, but joy in the morning is even greater still!

I believe that at the dawning of the morning, the good Lord will ask of me a question or two. He will say, as I imagine it, "Dear Don, have you been faithful? I have sent you out on a journey to deliver the joyful news. Have you preached the true Word that I have given to you?" Then I will say, "By your grace, dear Lord, I have told the people just what you asked me to. I assured them of your power to give them

---

27   Revelation 22:5
28   Psalm 16:11

Joy in the Night, and that *Except the Lord* build the house, their labor in building is in vain. I told them of the need to be *More than Just Virgins,* and that you are the good *Lord of the Loathsome Leper.* I told them you sent them *An Invitation to Tarry* and how you suffered for them at *The Little Red Spot.* I told them that you have provided *An Oasis for a Tired Heart,* and I shared David's testimony of *Horrible Pits and New Songs.* I reminded them of the reality of *The Word Made Flesh,* and I preached of the blessed hope of *Joy in the Morning."*

Then it is my belief that the Lord will say, "Well done, thou good and faithful servant; enter thou into the joy of thy Lord." Notice what He says: "Enter … the joy." Oh, what a time that will be when I shall enter into that joy! Then my joy will not only be on the inside but also on the outside. I will not have joy only in my heart but also in my environs. Then, for the first time, I shall know what is that "fullness of joy," and I will fully understand the bliss of "pleasures forevermore." So, joy in the night is the joy that enters me now, and joy in the morning is the joy into which I shall *enter* then. We praise the Lord for the joy He gives in the night, but we wait with bated breath for the fuller joy that is to come in that morning!

It will be joy when I walk down those streets of pure gold; it will be joy when I am welcomed into the heavenly fold. What a joy when I lift up my voice to sing glory and honor to the eternal King!

I went down to Belize City with my friend, Evangelist Braham, some time ago. We pitched a tent in the heart of that Central American metropolis. For two weeks it was filled with hundreds of eager listeners who came out in droves to drink from the fountain of the living Word. I remember that on the final night he spoke about the morning. I heard the exclamations of hope and joy as men, women, and children were told: "In that morning there will be no sorrowful singing. In that morning there will be no sighing soul. In that morning there will be no gunshots ringing. In that morning all our worries shall be gone."[29]

As I ponder the glorious dawning of that never-ending day, my mind is brought back to that memorable Week of Prayer meeting at my alma mater around the year 2000. The speaker inspired us all with his beautiful representations of Christ, and the precious hope that we have in Him. The theme for the week was quite appropriate: "Preparing a University for the Advent." During that week we were wonderfully re-minded of what to expect when the morning comes.

I cannot recall exactly how the preacher said it, but I will share with you the es-sence of the hope that he so inspiringly enounced. We were told that sin's long reign will be finally terminated. Evil will be subjugated. War and strife will be eliminated.

---

29 Paraphrase from Balvin Braham, IAD officer, sermon, Belize, Central America, 2007.

Sickness and pain will be eradicated. Satan and his demons will be annihilated. Death itself will be exterminated. The dead in Christ will be resurrected. We who are alive and remain will be translated. Life will be perpetuated. Victory will be commemorated. God's character will be vindicated. And the Sabbath will be celebrated.

All our problems will then be rectified, our vile passions purified, our sorrows cast aside, and our status forever clarified. Our devotion will be intensified. Our needs will be eternally satisfied. Our praise will be magnified. Our bodies will be glorified. Our power will be amplified, *and our joy will be multiplied.*[30]

Weeping may endure for a night, but the morning is coming. Trouble may endure for a night, but the morning is coming. Heartache may endure for a night, but the morning is coming, and in that morning there will be perpetual and unspeakable joy. I have decided to be there, and I desire the same for you. Let this be your decision and all-consuming determination.

---

30 Adapted from R. Clifford Jones, "Whatever Became of Sin?" sermon, Northern Caribbean University, Mandeville, Jamaica, 2000.

Epilogue

As one reflects upon the events that transpired at the inception of the proclamation of this gospel by the apostles of Christ, it is remarkable to trace the mighty moving of the Holy Spirit. It is also amazing to recognize the powerful way in which God's chosen instruments were used to spread abroad the joyful news of a risen Savior. Yet even more remarkable shall be the manifestation of divine providence as the end of all things draws nigh, and this gospel of the kingdom is taken to every corner of the globe. Indeed, this journey has opened the eyes of the writer to the reality that God is already moving marvelously to draw men and women from darkness to His glorious light.

This book provides but a passing glance at God's wonderful work through the ministry of the author in his missionary expeditions. There have been, as the reader would have imagined, many other "stops along the journey," which are more than worthy of being treated in a chapter of their own, and their exclusion from this compilation is by no means a reflection on the relative importance of those encounters in the mind of the preacher.

It must be made clear to all that the experiences shared in this document would not have been possible without the persistent prayers, faithful friendship, and selfless support of godly persons in places like Bushy Park, Frome, May Pen, Braeton, Richmond, Mandeville, Dover, Gordon Town, and Chapelton, Clarendon, a place certainly closer to home and to the heart. The author recognizes the inestimable value of the encounters experienced at each of those "stops," and he sends out his heartfelt gratitude to those who have faithfully kept this cause before the Lord, especially in the trying hours of "the night" when friends are few and fidelity is found in scant supply.

For now, we continue our journey. There are yet many stops to make and many obstacles to overcome in our march toward the morning. After several years of living among and ministering to the Hispanic people in Mexico and Central America, the impression of the great need that exists for the living bread is only deeper. A forthcoming second volume is designed to address more directly the progress of the gospel project in this particular field.

It is the author's sincere hope that the blessing expressed at the beginning of this report has become a reality for all who have taken the time to accompany him on this short journey. May our voyage through the "night" lead us all to that final, most glorious destination—the golden "morning," whose approach is faster than many are ready to believe. *Joy in the Night* is a practical possibility and *joy in the morning* an imminent certainty!

We invite you to view the complete
selection of titles we publish at:

www.TEACHServices.com

Scan with your mobile
device to go directly
to our website.

Please write or e-mail us your praises, reactions, or
thoughts about this or any other book we publish at:

TEACH Services, Inc.
P U B L I S H I N G
www.TEACHServices.com • (800) 367-1844

P.O. Box 954
Ringgold, GA 30736

info@TEACHServices.com

TEACH Services, Inc., titles may be purchased in bulk for
educational, business, fund-raising, or sales promotional use.
For information, please e-mail:

BulkSales@TEACHServices.com

Finally, if you are interested in seeing
your own book in print, please contact us at

publishing@TEACHServices.com

We would be happy to review your manuscript for free.

CPSIA information can be obtained at www.ICGtesting.com
Printed in the USA
LVOW08s1430040514

384321LV00003B/149/P